First published in 2023 by Sm
www.smartgu

Copyright © 2023 Elizabeth Cook

The right of Elizabeth Cooke to be identified as the
accordance with Copyright, De

All rights reserved. You are granted permission to: make personal, non-commercial photocopies of
limited portions of the guide for your own study purposes; quote brief excerpts from the guide in
academic papers or presentations, with proper citation.

Any other use of this material, including reproduction, modification, distribution, or transmission
in whole or in part, without prior written permission from the copyright holder, is strictly
prohibited.

CW00386288

Title cover artwork credit: Midjourney

SMART GUIDES
Study tools for **extraordinary** minds.

TABLE OF CONTENTS

INTRODUCTION TO THIS STUDY GUIDE

About this study guide

The purpose of this study guide is to equip students with a comprehensive understanding of the AQA GCSE 'Worlds and lives' poetry anthology to be taught for the first time in 2023. In addition to conducting a detailed thematic and stylistic analysis of each poem, the guide offers a thorough contextual overview of the cultural and historical backdrop against which the works were written. The guide also offers a concise introduction to AQA's assessment objective, as well as sample exam questions and model essay analysis and answers, illustrating how students might approach comparative poetry analysis.

Visit www.smartguides.org.uk to discover our wide range of free and paid study resources.

About Smart Guides

Smart Guides is a **pioneering new education brand**: we produce challenging, syllabus-optimised guides, resources and courses aimed at ambitious students who want to go one step further in their studies.

Our founder, **a first-class Oxford graduate** from a socially mobile background, understands the unique challenges faced by driven students. That's why she created Smart Guides: a research-backed learning platform designed to unlock students' academic potential.

And Smart Guides isn't just about getting good grades. It's also about:
- **Helping students to develop critical thinking skills** that will empower them beyond the confines of the classroom.
- **Building students' intellectual confidence and resilience to overcome academic challenges.**
- **Fueling students' intellectual curiosity** beyond pre-defined syllabuses and igniting a life-long love of learning.

KEY SKILLS FOR TOP PERFORMERS

Top performers should demonstrate:
- Critical, exploratory comparison
- Judicious use of precise references to support interpretation(s)
- Analysis of writer's methods with subject terminology used judiciously
- Exploration of effects of writer's methods to create meanings
- Exploration of idea/perspectives/contextual factors shown by specific, detailed links between context/text/task

Essay technique

(1) Understand the assessment objectives.
AO1: Read, understand and respond to texts. Students should be able to:
- maintain a critical style and develop an informed personal response
- use textual references, including quotations, to support and illustrate interpretations

AO2: Analyse the language, form and structure used by a writer to create meanings and effects, using relevant subject terminology where appropriate.

AO3: Show understanding of the relationships between texts and the contexts in which they were written.

(2) Spend 5-10 minutes planning.
A plan might include a brief outline of your introduction, 3 main points/arguments, quotes to support your arguments, relevant contextual points for each point, and a brief outline of your conclusion.

(3) Adopt the PEEL technique.

You may wish to adopt the 'PEEL' technique as a general guide to ensure that you provide a well-evidenced and clearly-structured analysis of the texts. Don't forget to add in historical, political or literary context!

P - Point, E - Example, E - Explanation, L - Link

Example: *Compare how poets present a sense of dissatisfaction with the world in 'England in 1819' and one other poem from 'Worlds and lives'.*

British Romanticism was marked, not only by a revolution in poets' understanding of art and its provenance and powers, but also by an accompanying period of societal and political upheaval that was defined by the Industrial Revolution, the rise of liberal movements, and the voicing of radical ideas. In the political sonnet 'England in 1819', these radical anti-monarchical ideas find explicit expression, as the speaker rails against the deep-rooted corruption of England's institutions. The one-sentence structure with its stack of subject clauses gives the sense of an unchecked, almost breathless anger, that will build until the poem's hopeful climax in the final two lines. The plosive alliteration of "blind in blood, without a blow", and the sibilant alliteration of "A people starv'd and stabb'd", provides further emphasis to each element of this litany of wrongs. Wordsworth's 'Lines Written in Early Spring', by contrast, takes a less political, and more metaphysical approach to man's dissatisfaction with the world.

Postcolonial theory

Metonymy Ambiguity Mimesis

Alliteration Sublime Allusion

Volta Ekphrasis Litotes
Zeugma

Bucolic Apostrophe
Hyperbole

Irony Verse

Imagery Allegory Dissonance

Motif

Consonance Spoken word

Assonance Stanza

Verisimilitude Négritude

Neologism

Aphorism

Tone Anaphora

Sonnet Couplet

Enjambment Rhyme

Caesura Symbol Cadence

Paradox Free verse Refrain

Antithesis Anthropomorphism

Romanticism
Personification Metaphor

Chiasmus Prose poem

Oxymoron
Onomatopoeia Pathetic fallacy

Persona
Stress Rhythm Simile Antithesis

'LINES WRITTEN IN EARLY SPRING,' WILLIAM WORDSWORTH

Contextual background

Wordsworth, born in 1770, was one of the early founders of English Romanticism. Romanticism was a literary and artistic movement that originated in Britain in the 1780s as a revolt against the Neoclassicism of the previous centuries. Neoclassicism constituted a revival and revision of the artistic ideals of classical Greece and Rome, and was characterised by an emphasis on form over content, emotional restraint and logic. Romanticism, by contrast, was marked by a celebration of subjectivity, nature, individualism, freedom from rules, and a fascination with the mythology of the middle ages.

Romanticism, as well as being a cultural and artistic movement, also took on social and political significance, rebelling against the social and political norms of the Enlightenment and the scientific rationalisation of nature. Notable English Romantics include William Wordsworth, Samuel Taylor Coleridge, Lord Byron, Percy Bysshe Shelley, and John Keats.

Introduction to the poem

'Lines Written in Early Spring' is a *modified* lyrical ballad that explores man's relationship to nature. It is organised in a tightly structured verse form, with each stanza composed of three lines of iambic tetrameter, followed by a final line of iambic trimeter. Each stanza observes an ABAB rhyme scheme. The poem exhibits simple diction, direct address, and a veiled didacticism in purpose.

Key thematic features

The speaker's kinship with nature: *"To her fair works did Nature link/The human soul that through me ran"*. Throughout the poem, the speaker achieves a sympathetic identification with nature, saying, for example, that the least motion of the birds around him becomes *"a thrill of pleasure"* through his nervous system. Wordsworth, like fellow Romanticist Coleridge, believed that nature was the appropriate medium through which the "infinite" would be revealed to man.

Man's deviation from "Nature's holy plan": The speaker introduces a jarring note of dissonance, as he recognises how humankind has rejected this mystical interdependence or shared consciousness between man and nature. In this sense, the recurring line *"What man has made of man"* functions as a *volta* – a rhetorical shift or dramatic change in the thought or direction of a poem.

Animism – that is, the attribution of a living soul to the inanimate and natural phenomena: *"And 'tis my faith that every flower/Enjoys the air it breathes."*

Doubt, ambiguity and uncertainty: The poem might seem to undermine its plea for belief in nature by its own uncertain discourse. It opens, for example, on the line, *"I heard a thousand blended notes,"* implying a confusion of voices. It is also interleaved with various tentative constructions: *"I must think, do all I can"*, *"It seemed"*, and *"And 'tis my faith."* The use of iambic trimeter in the final line of each stanza also brings special emphasis to the ambiguous, largely negative sentiment expressed therein: *"Bring sad thoughts to the mind"* and *"What man has made of man."* Like in Wordsworth's *Tintern Abbey*, there is an oscillation between the twin poles of certainty and speculation.

Key stylistic features

Metaphor: Wordsworth spoke of poetry as "a certain colouring of the imagination, whereby ordinary things should be presented to the mind in an unusual way", which, in this case, is achieved by a number of personifying metaphors, e.g., *"The budding twigs spread out their fan"*. Many critics attribute this to Wordsworth belief in an "anima mundi" – a psyche of the universe, which is the source of all being. In *Tintern Abbey*, he writes of *"A motion and a spirit, that impels/All thinking things, all objects of all thought,/And rolls through all things."*

Allusive: The poem was written amidst the French Revolutionary Wars of 1792 to 1802, which after 1800 merged into the Napoleonic Wars that lasted until 1815. Once an eager partisan of the Revolution, Wordsworth's enthusiasm for regime change quickly transformed into disillusionment. The line *"What man has made of man"* seems a clear reference to this disillusionment.

Movement from the particular to the general: Wordworth's poems are often anchored by way of a carefully observed scene, and these descriptive particularities will usually engender broader, general statements, with universal application. The final stanza displays this generality in its lament for man's deviation from *"Nature's holy plan"*.

Polarities or antithesis: Emphasised by the ABAB rhyme scheme, the poem is organised around various thematic and stylistic polarities. Although the poem flirts with the idea of a man in harmony with nature, there is the implication that the external world remains impenetrable: *"Their thoughts I cannot measure"*. The line, *"To her fair works did Nature link/The human soul that through me ran"*, also seems to be jeopardised by the enjambment that separates "Nature" from the human soul. In the final stanza, there is this same juxtaposition of the divine and man.

Narrative and discursive speech planes: On the one hand, the speaker is narrating an experience of nature in early spring, and on the other, he frequently signals his participation in a discursive mode of discourse, by introducing the conditional mood: *"If this belief from heaven be sent/If such be Nature's holy plan"*, etc. Anaphora in these lines, with the repetition of 'If', underlines the poet's inability to ascertain the validity of his mystical insights.

Iambic trimeter in the stanzas' final line: The single line of iambic trimeter at the end of each stanza, two syllables short of the previous three lines, unseats the expectations of the ballad form.

Exercise

Read the following analysis of 'Lines Written in Early Spring' by the critic Adam Potkay:

"Wordsworth works both **within and against the phonic expectations of the form**, and does so with a craftsmanship that involves by his own account "a more impressive metre than is usual in Ballads" (Prose Works 150). The modified ballad stanza of "Lines written in Early Spring," a stanza of 8, 8, 8, and then 6 syllables, draws attention to the last line by having it come up short. The **thematic surprises** of this poem unfold in **stanzas that end on notes of mystery**—what are those "sad thoughts"? What "has man made of man?" These successive mysteries unfold in curtailed lines of six rather than eight syllables, so that as we come to the end of each stanza, we have **a rhythmic as well as semantic sense of something missing**."

Credit: 'Captivation and Liberty in Wordsworth's Poems on Music', Adam Potkay

Read the following analysis of Wordsworth's poetic aesthetic by Thomas Jackson:

"Like the poetic theory of other major poets of his day, Wordsworth's centres upon the importance of significant things—**the meaning in natural objects**, "primal sympathies" among men, the Magnificent Personality of the Poet—and upon poetry as the transmission not quite of the things themselves, but of **the poet's experience of these things**."

Credit: 'Wordsworth's "Thought" and His Verse', Thomas H. Jackson

How could you incorporate insights or quotes from these critics into an analysis of Wordsworth's 'Lines Written in Early Spring'?

Contextual background

Percy Bysshe Shelley (1792-1822) was a British Romantic poet and philosopher known for his radical political and social views, as well as his unconventional personal life. He was born into a wealthy aristocratic family and was educated at Eton and Oxford. He was expelled from the latter for his atheistic beliefs and his publication of a pamphlet called "The Necessity of Atheism."

Shelley's poetry is marked by his idealistic and revolutionary vision, as well as his interest in nature, beauty, and the supernatural. His best-known works include 'Ode to the West Wind,' 'Prometheus Unbound,' and 'Ozymandias.' He also wrote the essay, 'Defense of Poetry', a kind of introduction to the motivating principles of Romanticism. There, he writes that, "Poetry lifts the veil from the hidden beauty of the world," and "Poets are the unacknowledged legislators of the world." He also champions the utilitarian function of poetry, insofar as he believes that it "awakens and enlarges the mind itself by rendering it the receptacle of a thousand unapprehended combinations of thought."

Introduction to the poem

'England in 1819' is a political sonnet, metered in iambic pentameter, that makes frequent allusions to contemporary events. The title refers to the Peterloo Massacre, which took place at St Peter's Field, Manchester, on 16th August 1819.

After the Napoleonic Wars in 1815, there was an acute economic depression that was exacerbated by chronic unemployment, harvest failure, the Corn Laws and highly restricted suffrage. At the time, only around eleven percent of men had the right to vote, very few of whom lived in the industrial North. Following a failed campaign for manhood suffrage, the Manchester Patriotic Union organised a mass rally, addressed by the radical orator and agitator, Henry Hunt. The Manchester and Salford Yeomanry were called upon to arrest Hunt, and the 15th The King's Hussars, a cavalry regiment, were called upon to disperse the crowd. Charging with sabres drawn, contemporary reports estimated that approximately 9-17 people were killed and 400-700 injured.

Key thematic features

Social ideals and revolutionary hopes: The litany of the age's worst excesses and evils will culminate on a note of optimism: the despised King (King George III), the scorned princes, the despotic army, the Godless religion and the unrepealed laws, are all *"graves from which a glorious Phantom may/Burst, to illumine our tempestuous day."* In other words, the injustices of the day will, it is hoped, become a spur to action. The poem does not call for peaceable social change, but is filled with violent hope: victory will arrive on *"our tempestuous day"*.

The ambivalence of idealism: The whole poem hinges on the word *"may"* in the penultimate line. Indeed, the speaker is identifying a historical moment that is full of ambiguities: the British government is either on the brink of collapse, or will become more entrenched than ever, bolstered by its army, religion, and judiciary.

Historically self-reflective: Romanticism has been characterised as a period when the normative status of the period becomes a central and self-conscious aspect of historical reflection. The critic, James Chandler, has even argued that 1819 was the moment that changed the conception of history itself, as political debate shifted from the 1790s' "threshold distinctions – reason/passion, liberty/slavery, state of nature/state of civil society, nature/second nature" to "arguments about historical movements, historical necessities, epochs, and formation." He argues that English writers active in 1819 became conscious of themselves, not only as participants in quotidian experience, but also as agents in that larger, formalized landscape called "history".

King George III reigned from 1760 until his death in 1820

Key stylistic features

Composed of one sentence: The poem contains just one sentence, with its main verb, *"Are"*, delayed until line 13. All the lines before this verb form a catalogue of England's vices, forming a compound subject that will at last be overthrown by that optimistic finale.

Structural features: The list of England's evils does not proceed from bad to worse as might be expected, but proceeds from the wellspring of those evils – the *"old, mad, blind, despis'd, and dying king"*, or George III, whose Hanoverian bloodline pollutes everything that it touches, like *"mud from a muddy spring."* The implication, perhaps, is that England's moral order is topsy-turvy.

Allusive: The opening reference to *"An old, mad, blind, despis'd, and dying king"* brings to mind Shakespeare's tragedy, *King Lear*, in which the king goes figuratively blind and literally mad.

Polyvalent: Polyvalent in this context means to have many different facets and meanings. For example, the poet speaks of *"Golden and sanguine laws"*, which might carry multiple meanings. "Golden" is ironic to the extent that England's laws violate ordinary morality, literal to the extent that England's laws serve the interests of the gilded moneyed class, and allusive to the extent that it may refer to the Golden Calf – an idol or cult image made by the Israelites when Moses went up to Mount Sinai. "Sanguine" is also an over-determined signifier, deriving from the Latin for "blood", as well as meaning optimistic or hopeful. The reference to *"A people starved and stabbed in th' untilled field"* is also ambiguous: the "field" could refer to St Peter's, or to all the English fields left "untilled" after the Corn Laws.

Plosive alliteration: The abundance of plosive consonants in the sixth line (*"Till they drop, blind in blood, without a blow"*) produces a series of explosive sounds, lending emphasis to the poem's pent-up sense of injustice and anger.

Exercise

What does the "glorious Phantom" represent? A phantom of what?
A phantom of liberty or justice, long-dead and long-denied to the people?
Perhaps this is left deliberately unspecified – victory is phantasmal because
it has not yet taken material form.

'England in 1819' is written in sonnet form. What is the significance of this?
The Romantic poets, inspired by Milton's political sonnets, revived and
repurposed the sonnet form for public and political utterances,
paradoxically co-opting a conventional form for unconventional content.

What other poems in the anthology could 'England in 1819' be compared to?
What themes do the poems have in common?
- Wordsworth's 'Lines Written in Early Spring' - A shared dissatisfaction
  and disillusionment with the world?
- Eliot's 'In a London Drawingroom' - A shared concern with England's
  social and political conditions?
- Dharker's 'A Century Later'? Both contain imagery of ideologically-
  motivated violence and bloodshed, while voicing a resounding note of
  defiance and resistance in the face of injustice.

AO2 specifies that students should "analyse the language, form and
structure used by a writer to create meanings and effects". This means that
judicious, purposeful references to the poem's language, form and
structure will be rewarded more highly than those that do not support an
interpretation of the poem's meaning.

Contextual background

Emily Brontë (1818-1848) was a Yorkshire-born English novelist and poet. She was the fifth of six children, and grew up in her father's parsonage on the isolated, windswept moors of Haworth alongside her siblings (including famous sisters Charlotte and Anne Brontë).

Her only novel, Wuthering Heights (1847), embodies the characteristic spirit of English Romanticism and Gothicism, telling a story of unbridled human passion and obsession, and the desire to transcend the limitations of the body, of society, and of time.

Emily's other major work is a collection of poetry, published alongside her sisters' works as Poems by Currer, Ellis, and Acton Bell (1846). Her poetry is, aesthetically and ideologically, of a piece with her novel, and explores many of the same ideas: the imagination's power to achieve extreme states of being, nature as a vitalising force and a refuge from civilisation, making society and its dictates peripheral to the action, and the individual as a source of intense subjective experience.

Introduction to the poem

'Shall earth no more inspire thee' takes the form of a dramatic monologue, in which the lyrical speaker is Earth, and the human listener remains silent. The speaker's words are persuasive and cajoling, and call on the listener to reconcile with her after a period of spiritual absence ("I've seen thy spirit bending/In fond idolatry.").

There may also appear to be an implicit sense of threat in the poem, as the speaker (Earth) asserts its "mighty sway" and "magic power": *"I've watched thee every hour;/I know my mighty sway,/I know my magic power/ To drive thy griefs away."* As in Wuthering Heights, "Nature" is presented, not just in its calm, tranquil aspects that Wordsworth is wont to represent, but also in its powerful, moody and mercurial aspects.

Brontë's poetic works have often been credited with ousting the traditional monotheistic Christian model of the universe, in favour of Nature worship, and here, Nature becomes a godly or spiritual presence, being endowed with the divine characteristics of omniscience and omnipotence. Similarly, heaven is envisioned as just another earth: *"Yet none would ask a heaven/More like this earth than thine."* In this way, Brontë's poem upholds the familiar Romantic idea that sublime nature is, if not superior to, more divine than man-made culture.

The birthplace of the Brontë sisters – Haworth, West Yorkshire

Key thematic features

The all-powerful, vitalising character of Earth: The speaker claims to be all-powerful and all-knowledgeable, exerting control over the listener when their wills come into conflict. Readers may even detect slightly menacing undertones in the cajoling nature of the speaker and their claims to godliness. This same representation of nature – as a balm for the soul, with a forbidding undercurrent – plays out in Brontë's *Wuthering Heights*, where sublime nature is wild, frightening, and awe-inspiring. This Romantic idea of the sublime is commonly thought to have derived from political philosopher, Edmund Burke, whose *Philosophical Enquiry* (1757) connected the sublime with experiences of awe, terror and danger.

Key stylistic features

Persuasive language: The poem is a plea for the listener to take solace in the natural world, and is replete with numerous persuasive rhetorical techniques, including rhetorical questions, direct injunctions (*"Return and dwell with me"*), and repetition (e.g. *"Shall"*).

Lilting rhythm: Written in iambic tetrameter, the poem creates a lilting rhythm, mimicking the evoked effect of the Earth's breeze on the listener (*"I know my mountain breezes/ Enchant and soothe thee still"*, *"Then let my winds caress thee"*, etc.) Sibilance (e.g. *'Sinks from the summer sky'*) reinforces the hushed intimacy of the speaker's words.

Religious lexicon: The speaker takes on a divine character, making repeated claims to omnipotence and omniscience (e.g. in the fifth stanza). Fittingly, the poem employs a religious lexicon, claiming that the listener has indulged in *"idolatry"* and that the speaker alone can *"bless"* them.

Model comparative analysis

Example: *Compare how poets present man's relationship to nature in 'Shall earth no more inspire thee' and one other poem from 'Worlds and lives'.*

Brontë's 'Shall earth no more inspire thee' and Wordsworth's 'Lines Written in Early Spring' are alike in promoting the familiar **Romantic** idea that the **sublime**—the awe-inspiring, often frightening, beauty of nature—is a balm to men's souls, while indulging in a shared objection to man-made culture. Both **deify** nature by investing it with divine properties: while 'Lines Written in Early Spring' speaks of *"Nature's holy plan"* and **capitalises** the word in a sign of holy reverence, Brontë's speaker (nature or earth itself) is endowed with divine characteristics of omnipotence and omniscience: *"I've watched thee every hour;/I know my mighty sway"*, etc. This **deification and personification** of nature reflects a shared objection amongst the great Romantic poets to the **scientific rationalisation of nature**, to the mechanistic universe, as envisaged by Newton; nature, they wanted to believe, is an organic whole – something that is continuous with moral and aesthetic values, rather than atomistic and entirely reducible to scientific abstractions.

Literary context and a point of comparison is immediately drawn out

Microscopic analysis of language and poetic techniques draws out how meaning is created in the poems

Use of relevant subject terminology

More literary and cultural context adds depth to the response and is used to elucidate the poets' choices

However, Wordsworth's poem might be said to adopt a more distinctly **metaphysical or philosophical approach** to the concept of "Nature" than 'Shall earth no more inspire thee', seeing it as begetting a now lost, undistorted human nature: *"To her fair works did Nature link/ The human soul that through me ran;/ And much it grieved my heart to think/ What man has made of man."* The final **stanza** also takes the form of a **rhetorical question**, creating an atmosphere of philosophical contemplation, whilst 'Shall earth no more inspire thee' ends as it began – on a note of **rhetorical pathos.** While the latter almost takes for granted man's spriritual connection to nature, 'Lines Written in Early Spring' attest to the difficulties of recapturing this lost "link". While 'Shall earth no more inspire thee' contains four instances of verbs of certainty ("I know"), 'Lines Written in Early Spring' frequently signals its participation in a **discursive and uncertain mode of discourse**. It opens, for example, on the line, "I heard a thousand blended notes," implying a confusion of voices. It is also interleaved with various tentative constructions: "I must think, do all I can", "It seemed", and "And 'tis my faith." The use of **iambic trimeter** in the final line of each stanza also brings special emphasis to the ambiguous, largely negative sentiment expressed therein: "Bring sad thoughts to the mind" and "What man has made of man."

The poems are compared and contrasted consistently throughout the response

Analysis of meaning is conducted through careful evaluation of poetic techniques

The purpose of poetic structure and metre is drawn out

This tendency towards abstract discursiveness in Wordsworth may also reflect the fact that he had **a more well-developed theory of nature than Brontë**, believing it to be pervaded with a divine *anima* and able to enter moral communion with man. Wordsworth's ideation about man's relationship to nature took shape most clearly in the poem "Tintern Abbey". There, he described the *"spirit, that impels/All thinking thing, all objects of all thought,/And rolls through all things"*.

An interesting look at the poets' individual philosophies to explain differences in their poetic treatment of nature

⟶

What other points of comparison are there between 'Shall earth no more inspire thee' and 'Lines Written in Early Spring'?

- A shared view of the individual as a source of intense subjective experience
- Both are written in a lilting iambic foot, mimicking the swaying, soothing rhythms of nature
- A shared focus on the idealised poetic persona, with an abundance of first-person pronouns
- A shunning of man-made culture

'IN A LONDON DRAWINGROOM',
GEORGE ELIOT

Contextual background

George Eliot was the pen name of Mary Ann Evans (1819-1880), an English Victorian novelist, poet, and translator. She has been credited with developing the method of psychological analysis that characterises much modern fiction.

In 1859, she published her first full-length novel, *Adam Bede*, wherein she sets out her commitment to realism as a literary genre. In an essay on the artist and critic John Ruskin (1819-1900), Eliot herself defined realism as "the doctrine that all truth and beauty are to be attained by a humble and faithful study of nature." By this, she did not mean that art can transparently represent the world, but rather that it should not falsify or romanticise it. Indeed, she believed that realism imposed itself on the artist as a moral and aesthetic imperative. Realist art represents and dramatises the value of the ordinary: "Art," she wrote, "is the nearest thing to life; it is a mode of amplifying experience and extending our contact with our fellow men beyond the bounds of our personal lot. All the more sacred is the task of the artist when he undertakes to pain the life of the People."

Adam Bede frequently points towards its own methods of representation, and mocks the romanticist impulse to soften the hard edges of human life. With satirical contempt, she dismisses the injunction that if "The world is not just what we like; do touch it up with a tasteful pencil, and make believe it is not quite such a mixed, entangled affair."

She went on to write several other novels, including *The Mill on the Floss*, *Silas Marner*, *Middlemarch*, and *Daniel Deronda*. In all her novels, her characters' triumphs take the form of renunciations, or submissions in the face of conflict between individual desires and moral responsibility. There is also a determinist vein to her novels, underpinned by the belief that every individual can only be understood in relation to their social relationships. In Middlemarch, the narrator interjects: "But any one watching keenly the stealthy convergence of human lots, sees a slow preparation of effects from one life on another [...]"

Introduction to the poem

In George Eliot's 'In a London Drawingroom', setting serves to provide a snapshot of life in 1860s London. Written in iambic pentameter, the poem nevertheless feels like a spontaneous "bricolage" of impressions, featuring frequent enjambment and free verse. There is a sense of acute anonymity, both of the speaker and of the scene and people which she beholds – nothing is sharply particularised or described, but is grouped in with a collective.

At the time of writing (1869), industrialisation had reached its zenith, bringing a high level of mechanisation, manufacturing output, and industrial employment, and attracting the majority of the population into urban centres. From approximately 1.4 million people in 1815, the population of Greater London grew to well over 3 million by 1860. This new metropolis brought diverse classes, cultures, vocations and linguistic groups into close proximity, hollowing out traditional social bonds and eroding the natural rhythms of production. It is against this climate of modernity that Eliot wrote 'In a London Drawingroom', with Charles Baudelaire, the French Symbolist poet, defining "modernity" as "the transitory, the fugitive, the contingent, that half of art of which the other is the eternal and immutable". The fugitive and transitory, as we will see, features heavily in 'In a London Drawingroom'. The poem has been considered unique amongst Eliot's works insofar as it turns upon the nature of the world perceived, and not upon the way in which the speaking consciousness perceives it. In other words, the poem is pre-conceptual; the images stand alone, rather than serving to illustrate a thought.

Key thematic features

The transitory and the fugitive: The transitory, ephemeral nature of contemporary life features heavily in the poem, e.g. *"No figure lingering/Pauses to feed the hunger of the eye"*, and *"All hurry on & look upon the ground,/Or glance unmarking at the passers by/The wheels are hurrying too, cabs, carriages"*.

The monotony and uniformity imposed by urbanisation: The poem speaks of the people, vehicles and houses of London as being *"closed, in multiplied identity"*; everyone is assimilated into one single entity by their living conditions and the frenetic pace of daily life. The poem mirrors this monotony is its own form and content, with a conversational rhythm and a dearth of lyrical or figurative language.

The suppression of the natural world: Elements of the natural world are blotted out by the thick smog and shadow of 1860s London. The sky, that universal symbol of freedom and infinity, is *"cloudy, yellowed by the smoke"*, whilst birds cannot make shadows as they fly, and the golden rays of the sun *"Are clothed in hemp"*.

Key stylistic features

Similes: All the poem's similes reflect unfavourably upon London's living conditions, and the poem aptly concludes by comparing the urban scene to *"one huge prison-house and court/Where men are punished at the slightest cost"*.

Focus on mundane details: In *Adam Bede*, Eliot embraces a literary gaze that turns "without shrinking, from cloud-borne angels, from prophets, sibyls, and heroic warriors, to an old woman bending over her flower pot, or eating her solitary dinner [..]". In other words, she is concerned with the sublimity of monotony and the everyday. In 'In a London Drawingroom', we have a proliferation of these mundane details.

Lexicon of enclosure/entrapment: There is an abundance of lexical items conveying enclosure or entrapment: *'one long line of wall'*, *'solid fog'*, *'thickest canvas'*, *'All closed'*, *'one huge prison-house'*.

Enjambment: The poem's enjambment dulls any rhythmic impetus in a way that conveys the dullness and uniformity of the capital and the people therein. For example, the long run-on line, *'For view there are the houses opposite/Cutting the sky with one long line of wall/Like solid fog'*, is more prosaic than poetic. The single stanza form, written in blank verse, might seem to mirror the fifth line: *"Monotony of surface & of form"*.

Exercise

Read the following extract from Friedrich Engels' *Condition of the Working Class in England*, written in 1845:

"A town, such as London, where a man may wander for hours together **without reaching the beginning of the end**, without meeting the slightest hint which could lead to the inference that there is open country within reach, is a strange thing. This colossal centralisation, this heaping together of two and a half millions of human beings at one point, has multiplied the power of this two and a half millions a hundredfold; has raised London to the commercial capital of the world, created the giant docks and assembled the thousand vessels that continually cover the Thames. [...]

After roaming the streets of the capital a day or two, making headway with difficulty through the human turmoil and the endless lines of vehicles, after visiting the slums of the metropolis, one realises for the first time that these Londoners have been forced to **sacrifice the best qualities of their human nature**, to bring to pass all the marvels of civilisation which crowd their city; that a hundred powers which slumbered within them have remained inactive, have been suppressed in order that a few might be developed more fully and multiply through union with those of others. The very turmoil of the streets has something repulsive, something against which human nature rebels.

The hundreds of thousands of all classes and ranks crowding past each other, are they not all human beings with the same qualities and powers, and with the same interest in being happy? And have they not, in the end, to seek happiness in the same way, by the same means? And **still they crowd by one another as though they had nothing in common**, nothing to do with one another, and their only agreement is the tacit one, that each keep to his own side of the pavement, so as not to delay the opposing streams of the crowd, while it occurs to no man to honour another with so much as a glance. The **brutal indifference, the unfeeling isolation** of each in his private interest, becomes the more repellent and offensive, the more these individuals are crowded together, within a limited space."

How does Engels' description of London echo Eliot's depiction in 'In A London Drawingroom'?

Model comparative analysis

Example: *Compare how poets present the shaping of lives by social and political conditions in 'In a London Drawingroom' and one other poem from 'Worlds and lives'.*

Eliot's 'In a London Drawingroom' and Shelley's 'England in 1819' express a discontent with **the unjust social and political condition of the 19th century Britain,** albeit in very different ways. The latter takes the form of an impassioned, even revolutionary, condemnation of the state of Britain under the rule of King George III, whose leadership is cast as the wellspring of the country's evils. This poetic insurrection derives its **rhetorical power** from the breathlessness of its **two run-on sentence structure**, its **plosive and sibilant alliteration**, and its **highly-charged imagery**: "leechlike", "a muddy spring", "blind in blood", and "starved and stabbed in th' untilled field". The critic, Northrop Frye, even went so far as to claim that there is a **utopian or revolutionary quality inherent in Romanticism**, given its idealism and its "polarizing between two worlds, one desirable and the other hateful". 'In a London Drawingroom', by contrast, consists in an **impassive description** of the smog-filled, alienating conditions of Victorian London, whose **tone** is more one of resignation than of revolutionary insurrection. For example, the poem is replete with **images of entrapment and enclosure**: "The sky is cloudy", "For view there are the houses opposite", "All closed", and "The world seems one huge prison-house & court". And, unlike 'England in 1819', which culminates on an **image of revolutionary hope**, Eliot's poem ends on **a triad of denied abstract nouns**: "With lowest rate of colour, warmth & joy".

Both poems are grounded by some form of spatio-temporal specificity: 'In a London Drawingroom' is the description of a scene viewed from a London drawingroom, while 'England in 1819' is rooted in the specific socio-political context of 1819 – the year of the Peterloo Massacre. Indeed, Romanticism has been characterised as a period when the normative status of the period becomes a central and self-conscious aspect of historical reflection. The critic, James Chandler, has argued that 1819 marked a moment when English writers became conscious of themselves, not only as participants in quotidian experience, but also as agents in that larger, formalized landscape called "history". In 'England in 1819', one can detect the poet's overarching concern with the movement of history: the poem is a **building list** of England's failing institutions (King, the Crown, Parliament, the army, the legislators, and the Church) that will lay the groundwork for a new epoch. Eliot's concern for her social environment, by contrast, reflects the strong strain of **realist writing** that was dominating European literature in the mid-19th century, which aimed at reproducing quotidian experience without the mediation of interpretation. Literary critic, Ian Watt, makes the case in *The Rise of the Novel* that **modern realism** "begins from the position that truth can be discovered by the individual through the senses" and as such "has its origins in Descartes and Locke, and received its full formulation by Thomas Reid in the middle of the eighteenth century." 'In a London Drawingroom' is composed entirely of **true-to-life or *mimetic* description**, with one sole element of interpretation or judgment at the poem's end: "*The world seems one huge prison-house & court/Where men are punished at the slightest cost*".

Structurally, the poems share the same **single-stanza form** and feature heavy use of **enjambment**. The use of the single-stanza **sonnet form** in 'England in 1819' reflects a wider trend amongst the Romantics who, following Milton, regularly co-opted this conventional poetic form for public and political utterances. In 'In a London Drawingroom', form echoes content: the use of blank verse may seem to mirror the poem's fifth line's description ("Monotony of surface & of form.")

Notice the turns of phrase, highlighted in green, which signal that a comparison is being made. These signposting techniques help the examiner see how similarities and differences are being drawn out.

27

A schematic timeline of literary movements in English literature

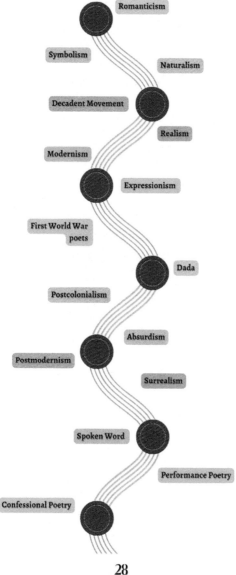

Romanticism

Symbolism

Naturalism

Decadent Movement

Realism

Modernism

Expressionism

First World War poets

Dada

Postcolonialism

Absurdism

Postmodernism

Surrealism

Spoken Word

Performance Poetry

Confessional Poetry

Trends in post-1950s literature

Most of the poems in the collection were written post-1950 – a time of immense political and social upheaval, which bore witness to the Cold War's head-on collision between capitalism and communism, the civil rights movement, demographic changes, the sexual revolution, and the beginning of decolonisation across Africa and Asia.

In the arts, the 1950s heralded the birth of the intellectual and artistic mode of discourse *postmodernism,* a product of the historical period of *postmodernity.* Scholar Terry Eagleton defines "postmodernism" as "a style of thought which is suspicious of classical notions of truth, reason, identity and objectivity, of the idea of universal progress or emancipation, of single frameworks, grand narratives or ultimate grounds of explanation. Against these Enlightenment norms, it sees the world as contingent, ungrounded, diverse, unstable, indeterminate, a set of disunified cultures or interpretations which breed a degree of scepticism about the objectivity of truth, history and norms, the givenness of natures and the coherence of identities."

Postcolonialism, a cherished orthodoxy of the postmodernists, also emerged as a mode of intellectual and aesthetic discourse, taking the imperialist subject as a space to criticise Western post-industrial culture and the totalising manifestations of the European. Postcolonialist themes can be detected in 'On an Afternoon Train from Purley to Victoria', 'Name Journeys' and 'pot', whose subjects are of non-European descent and which describe the experience of living in the intersection between non-European cultures and Western colonialism.

> **"**
>
> **Terry Eagleton on postmodernism:**
>
> "[It is] a style of thought which is suspicious of classical notions of truth, reason, identity and objectivity, of the idea of universal progress or emancipation, of single frameworks, grand narratives or ultimate grounds of explanation [...]"
>
> **"**

Scholar Ankhi Mukherjee notes that the postcolonialist poet often appropriates the Western literary canon for the narration of their own emancipation or repression. This "conscious or unconscious affiliation and allusiveness to the Western literary tradition", she says, "is an inheritance that is often as unwanted as it is laboured for." This "allusiveness" can be detected in 'A Century Later', and to a lesser extent, in 'A Portable Paradise', where marginalised peoples co-opt familiar poetic forms, symbols or narratives to empower their own stories.

Confessionalism (often classified as a sub-genre of postmodernism) also emerged in the late 1950s and early 60s as a style of poetry that turned away from the social realities of the mid-20th century and towards traumatic autobiographical experiences. We might hear stylistic and thematic echoes of confessionalism in poems such as 'Name Journeys', 'Thirteen', and 'Homing'. Like the archetypal confessionalist poets (Sylvia Plath, Robert Lowell, etc.), these poems jettison the traditional, idealised poetic persona (as might be found in 'Lines Written in Early Spring'), and instead create a speaker, an 'I', who can connect with the audience on a more intimate level, while speaker and poet become conflated. Thematically, confessionalist poetry is often concerned with taboo autobiographic experience, the self, and revelations of both childhood and adult traumas – themes which manifest in 'Thirteen' and 'Name Journeys'.

Charles Molesworth on confessional poetry:

"In a sense confessional poetry can be seen as one degraded branch of Romanticism, placing the sensitivity of the poet at the centre of concern. In other terms, it mockingly inverts the nineteenth-century ideals of "conversion" and "self-improvement," since an almost notion of inner light flickers against the morbid self-voyeurism the model exhibits."

Exercise

Read these critics' description of confessionalism, the genre of poetry that popularised the exploration of the self:

"For most contemporary critics, confessional poetry marked **a revolution in poetic style** as well as specific subject matter and the relationship between a poem's speaker and self. Confessional poets wrote in **direct, colloquial speech rhythms** and used images that reflected **intense psychological experiences**, often culled from childhood or battles with mental illness or breakdown. They tended to utilize sequences, emphasizing connections between poems. They grounded their work in actual events, referred to real persons, and **refused any metaphorical transformation of intimate details into universal symbols**. In the 1950s and 1960s, decades saturated with New Criticism dictates that the poet and "speaker" of a poem were never coincident, confessional poets insisted otherwise. Their **breaches in poetic and social decorum were linked**. According to scholar Deborah Nelson, Lowell's "**innovation was to make himself ... available, not as the abstract and universal poet but as a particular person in a particular place and time.**"

Credit: "An Introduction to Confessional Poetry", Poetry Foundation

As you make your way through the rest of the poetry anthology, make a note of which poems exhibit:
- "Direct, colloquial speech rhythms"
- "Images that [reflect] intense psychological experiences"
- "Images culled from childhood"
- "[A refusal of] any metaphorical transformation of intimate details into universal symbols"
- A conflation of the poet and speaker of the poem

Which contemporary poets might seem to buck this confessionalist trend? Does Shamshad Khan's 'pot', for example, refuse "any metaphorical transformation of intimate details into universal symbols"?

Contextual background

James Berry was born on September 28, 1924, in rural Jamaica, growing up in a family reliant on subsistence farming and the sea. He emigrated to England in 1948 on a ship called SS Orbita. He was invited, along with many other West Indians, to join the depleted postwar labour force in Britain, becoming part of what is now known as the "Windrush generation". He continued, however, to draw literary inspiration from his early exposure to Jamaican folklore, language and traditions.

Berry's poetry explores the complexities of the immigrant experience, addressing themes such as colonialism, discrimination, and the search for belonging. In 1981, he would become the first West Indian poet to win the Poetry Society's National Poetry Competition.

Introduction to the poem

Written in 1955, 'On an Afternoon Train from Purley to Victoria' is one of Berry's earlier poems and conveys the sense of displacement or cultural dislocation that many West Indian migrants must have felt, as they confronted the ethnic and cultural homogeneity of post-war Britain. Depicting a brief conversation between the black Jamaican speaker and the white Quaker, the poem provides a fleeting glimpse into the growing pains of multicultural Britain.

Key thematic features

Discovery and newness: The setting of the poem – on a moving train – seems significant, and immediately places us within an atmosphere of movement and discovery. Ironically, however, the "native" is not really discovering, except through the lens of her own ignorance: *"Which part of Africa is Jamaica? she said."*

Nostalgia: There is a brief, unelaborated and "inexplicable" memory of *"empty city streets lit dimly/in a day's first hours"* and the speaker's *"father's big banana field"*. This memory might be a simple expression of nostalgia or longing for home, brought on by an alienating conversation, or the reference to his *"father's big banana field"* may more subtly evoke an industry that enabled the Jamaican people to break free from their country's colonial legacy. Liberated from the slave sugar plantation society and economy of the nineteenth century, ex-slaves and their descendants had worked to secure an independent existence through the acquisition of land and the banana trade. In this way, the poem may summon up a whole network of cultural references and meaning.

Communication or miscommunication: The poem captures the miscommunications and confusion of the host society, as it tries (but fails) to grasp the plurality and hidden dimensions of the world. Most damningly, the Quaker seems unaware of the European legacy of repression and subjection that brought black Africans to the West Indies in the 17th century. As Louis MacNeice said, "World is crazier and more of it than we think,/Incorrigibly plural." The speaker good-humouredly multiplies the woman's confusion further, with a grammatically and semantically meaningless statement : *"Where Ireland is near Lapland I said."*

Artwork credit: Midjourney

Forgiveness and harmony: The woman's ignorance seems to be forgiven as the speaker acknowledges her sincerity and seems moved by her beauty: *"So sincere she was beautiful/as people sat down around us."* This final image, of people gathered together on the train, all bound for the same destination, strikes an optimistic note, suggesting harmony and understanding.

Key stylistic features

Simple, unaffected writing style: The writing is simple and unaffected (*"Nice day. Nice day I agreed."*), emphasising the simplicity and unaffectedness of the interchange. It also brings special emphasis to that "inexplicable" image at the heart of the poem: the contrast of the empty city streets and the big banana field.

Irony: There is a vein of irony running through the poem: the Quaker makes a well-intended attempt to reach across racial divides, speaking *"a poem loudly/for racial brotherhood"*. However, one might wonder how worthwhile such a poem could be, given her ignorance of the culture and origins of her new compatriots.

Striking imagery: The poem contains several striking images, whose purpose is more to suggest and evoke a network of meanings, than to denote one single stable meaning. "Snow falls elsewhere" is a potent but obscure image, with its implications of woe, death and darkness, and possibly refers to the failure of Jamaica's post-colonial democracy – with its failure to address long-standing economic stagnation, poverty and violence. The poem's central image – *"empty city streets lit dimly/in a day's first hours"* and the *"big banana field"* – stand out for their resistance to straightforward interpretation.

Contextual background

Raman Mundair is an Indian-born British Asian writer who currently resides in Shetland and Glasgow. She characterises herself as an intersectional feminist and activist, having worked at a grassroots level on anti-racism, anti-facism, state violence, No Borders, and against gender-based, domestic and sexual violence. Her poetry is alive to these social and political issues, and features highly figurative and potent imagery. She focuses particularly on the experiences of people of colour, reframing these experiences from new and interesting perspectives. Mundair has denied that her poems are about alienation, preferring to see them as meditations on the outsider.

The critic Dr Devon Campbell-Hall says that "her poems resist William Connolly's assertion that "identity is what I am and how I am recognized rather than what I choose, want or consent to". This is a poet who unapologetically insists on being the maker, rather than the bearer, of meaning."

Introduction to the poem

'Name Journeys' is about how names, these important signifiers, come to bear meaning through rich "woven tapestries" of "history and memory". However, her name, loaded with cultural and historical significance, becomes "a stumble" and "a mystery" when transplanted into the mouths of English Mancunians. The poem, written in free verse, explores how identities take shape in this fraught encounter between individual subjectivities and the grand narratives of history and culture.

Key thematic features

Identity and the migrant experience: Mundair opens the poem by summoning up the Hindu deities Rama and Sita, situating herself and her identity within a culture that is profoundly foreign to the Global North. She also invokes other elements of Indian culture – its sugar canes, its banyan trees, and its silk industry – weaving them into her own sense of self. The cultural theorist Stuart Hall suggests that "identity is formed at the unstable point where the unspeakable stories of subjectivity meet the narratives of history, of a culture". Here, we have a head-on collision, as the poet's subjective sense of self encounters *"the Anglo echo chamber – / void of history and memory"*, which cannot make sense of her identity nor her name.

Language: The poem's linguistic proficiency, with its elevated semantic field (*chastened, entwined, interlacing, toiled, musicality, discordant*, etc.), shows a cultural and linguistic adaptability on the part of the poet, who "toils" to accommodate her adopted language and accent, that is missing on the part of the Mancunians: for them, her name becomes *"a stumble"*. The alliteration and assonance in the line, *"the rough musicality of Mancunian vowels"*, emphasises the effort expended in mastering the language. Language, like in Berry's 'Homing', becomes an outward sign of identity.

Scenes from the Ramayana in antique manuscript, Jaipur, Rajasthan, India

Key stylistic features

Allusions to Hinduism and broader Indian culture: The poem is highly allusive, referring to elements of Indian culture that might appear foreign and exotic to a European audience (e.g. the Hindu deities Rama and Sita, as well as the brief allusion to India's silk industry and Banyan trees). This serves to remind the reader of the role of history and culture in determining migrant identity, and jars against the censure of English culture as being *"void of history and memory"*. Sibilance in these lines on Indian culture, *"Sita and I,/spiritual sari-sisters entwined/in an infinite silk that would swathe..."*, conveys the effortlessness of cultural belonging.

Structural features (enjambment): Enjambment is cleverly used to reinforce meanings: for example, it brings emphasis to the fragmentation of identity imposed by *"travelling from South/to North"*. Enjambment also contributes to the semantic field of fracture and dislocation: *"where the Punjabi in my mouth/became dislodged as milk teeth fell/and hit infertile English soil."*

Unrhyming couplets: Unrhyming couplets convey both the aching desire for connection and the isolating reality of migration.

Harsh consonance: 'Name Journeys' contains lots of harsh consonant sounds (*"musicality"*, *"discordant"*, *"exotic"*), and *d* plosive sounds (*"dislodged"*, *"toiled"*, *"accommodate"*, *"filled"*, *"discordant"*, *"dulled"*, *"void"*), reflecting a barely concealed indignation and despair.

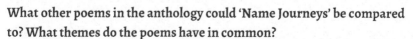

What other poems in the anthology could 'Name Journeys' be compared to? What themes do the poems have in common?

- Liz Berry's 'Homing' - A shared interest in how language and culture shapes our identities?
- James Berry's 'On an Afternoon Train from Purley to Victoria, 1955' - Interest in depicting the migrant experience?

Exercise

Read the following critic's review of Mundair's collection, *Lovers, Liars, Conjurers and Thieves*:

"An early piece within the collection, 'Name Journeys', outlines the fractured existence she felt as a migrant child,

travelling from South
to North, where the Punjabi in my mouth
became dislodged as milk teeth fell
and hit infertile English soil. (p 16)

There is nothing childlike in this collection, however, which would fit more comfortably into the category of 'womanist' than under the vague rubric of migrant literature. The cover photograph is of a dark-haired woman standing naked amongst a tangle of abandoned market stalls. She looks over her shoulder, as if to warn a younger self against the publishing industry's tendency to exoticize and commodify the writings of British Asian women.

[...] Mundair makes no excuses for the chaos of her first-generation identity. There is a resigned maturity about her voice, yet she maintains an unexpected sense of wonder. No topic is sacred, and readers get the feeling that there are no literary taboos under the steady, piercing gaze of her language. These poems stand in defiant rejection of the ordinary [...]"

How does Mundair represent "the chaos of her first-generation identity" in 'Name Journeys'?
- **Images of fracture and dislodgement**? "where the Punjabi in my mouth/became dislodged as milk teeth fell"
- **Enjambment** that brings emphasis to the fragmentation of identity? "travelling from South/to North"
- Her simultaneous **identification with and divergence from Indian culture** (her self-comparisons with Rama)

Model comparative analysis

Compare how poets present the migrant experience in 'Name Journeys' and one other poem from 'Worlds and lives'.

Berry's 'On an Afternoon Train from Purley to Victoria, 1955' and Mundair's 'Name Journeys' both explore the challenging, sometimes dislocating, experience of adapting to new cultures and new landscapes. Both poets write from **the perspective of having traveled from former British colonies** (Berry from Jamaica and Mundai from India) and encountered the astounding cultural and historical ignorance of the British. Berry lets this ignorance speak for itself with **direct speech**, while Mundair describes her experience through the mediation of normative judgment. To this extent, both poems are **confessional**, jettisoning the traditional idealised poetic persona and forefronting the **first-person "I"** to explore deeply personal and traumatic experiences. This confessionalism might be read as a postmodern deconstruction of power structures by deprioritising single narratives and **prioritising the voice of "the othered"**.

Both poems evoke the sense of **loss** that accompanies emigration by fond **allusions to their native culture**. In 'On an Afternoon Train', one central **image** stands out at the centre of the poem, book-ended by two more narratorial stanzas: the poet's father's *"big banana field"*. The image stands out for its **resistance to straightforward interpretation**, however may well refer to **Jamaica's post-colonial banana-growing industry,** which helped enable the Jamaican people to break free from their country's colonial legacy Mundai's 'Name Journeys' also invokes aspects of Indian culture, with **references to Hindu deities and the Indian landscape** (Banyan trees). At the poem's beginning, she at once locates herself within and separates herself from the iconography of her native culture, preparing us for the uprooting that she is about to undergo: *"Like Rama, I have felt the wilderness, but I have not been blessed with a companion as sweet as she [...]".*

However, while Berry's poem ends on a hopeful image of understanding, a coming together of people ("*So sincere she 'was beautiful/as people sat down around us.*"), all destined for the same city, Mundair's poem ends on a note of cynicism. On an Afternoon Train' adopts **a tone of gentle irony**, and in fact briefly gains ascendancy over his interlocutor, as he good-humouredly confuses her. By contrast, 'Name Journeys"s second half, replete with **harsh consonance**, builds a bleak picture of the dislocation and fragmentation of identity, as the speaker "*toils*" to assimilate into her adopted culture. **Images of fracture and dislodgement** ("*where the Punjabi in my mouth/became dislodged as milk teeth fell*") and **enjambment** ("*travelling from South/to North*") brings emphasis to the dislocating experience of emigrating to a country without any of the same cultural waymarkers. The cultural theorist Stuart Hall suggests that "identity is formed at the unstable point where the unspeakable stories of subjectivity meet the narratives of history, of a culture". Here, we have a head-on collision, as the poet's subjective sense of self encounters "*the Anglo echo chamber – / void of history and memory*", which cannot make sense of her identity nor her name.

Contextual background

Shamshad Khan (born 1964) is a Manchester-based poet of Pakistani heritage, whose work has been widely anthologised. She studied biology and animal behaviour at university, before becoming a secondary school science teacher.

Since 1998, she has been literary advisor to the North West Arts Board, and has co-edited a number of poetry anthologies. She was also a member of the Commonwealth project, Mushiara Shake-up, with the participation of women poets and artists from England, India and Pakistan.

Her poems, with their keen sense of rhythm and the spoken word, lend themselves well to performance, and Khan has participated in several shows, readings and stagings that combine soundtracks, contemporary dancers and musicians.

Introduction to the poem

The poem, dedicated to "all museum artefacts", raises questions about the status of museums as houses of appropriated (and often looted) artefacts, as well as broader issues around identity and the suppression of culturally diverse voices. Khan says that she "[uses] the pot as a way to comment on the issues of identity, colonial practices, migration and the slave trade."

It was written as a commission for the Manchester Museum.

Key thematic features

Identity: The poem centres on the embattled concept of identity – how it is formed, how it can be co-opted by others, how it can evolve and change and be *protean*. It is possibly significant that the artefact in question is a pot – an empty vessel that can be filled with different materials, and whose purpose can change (pots can be decorative as well as functional). The pot's value, however, derives not from its form (which resembles *"an english pot"*) or function, but from its emotional and sentimental connections: *"someone/somewhere will have missed you pot [...]"* In this way, the poet insists on the pot's (or the slave's) essential humanity.

Intercultural dialogue, empowering disempowered voices:
The poem might seem to call for intercultural dialogue, an opening of avenues for appropriated cultures to speak their truths. The distorting lens of Western colonialism has biased interpretation, softening and sweetening the story of the pot's origins, while suppressing its subjectivity (the sense of self as produced through cultural, political, linguistic and biological conditions). The West has invented a series of stories to justify the pot's "incarceration": *"did they say you were bought pot [...] did they say you were lost pot [...] did they say they didn't notice you pot [...]"* The poet, however, calls for the pot's history to be told in its own words: *"I know half of the story pot/of where you come from of how you got here/but I need you to tell me the rest pot"*. The pot, however, is notably silent at the poem's close, as the poet calls upon it to speak: *"empty pot/growl if you can hear me/pot? pot? pot."*

Cultural heritage and diaspora: As well as raising challenging questions about colonial wrongs, the pot also serves as a symbol of cultural heritage and diaspora (people of shared cultural and regional origins who have dispersed beyond their traditional homeland). At one point, the pot stands in as a poetic analogue for the poet herself, as she digresses to reflect upon her own origins and the homeland of her family: *"I've been back to where my family's from/they were happy/to see me/laughed a lot/said I was more asian than the asians pot"*. Her own origins and culture, she insists, are uncompromised by her also belonging to another country.

Migration and slavery: The pot serves as a vehicle for wider conversations about migration, and the movement of peoples and things across borders. Khan has said that the dedication at the end of the poem is designed to "[make] a further political comment in equating the placing of the pot in a museum with the incarceration of prisoners without access to legal representation and without charge."

Key stylistic features

Conversational tone and unorthodox punctuation: The rejection of literary conventions becomes the rejection of political conventions, with a notable absence of conventional punctuation (commas, capitalisation, etc.) or elevated lexis. The whole poem might be viewed as an upturning of the literary device of *ekphrasis* – the verbal (usually poetic) evocation of a piece of art. Here, however, the poet does not describe the pot, does not presume to tell its story, but rather calls upon it to tell its own story. Khan herself has said that the "conversational style" is designed to represent the direct address of the performer/poet to the pot.

Idioms and clichés: At one point, the poem ironically invokes the idiom, "finders keepers", in the line "finders are keepers you know pot", highlighting the moral clichés that colonialists have historically used to justify their wrongdoings.

Repetition/epistrophe: Epistrophe, or the repetition of "pot" at the end of successive lines, might seem to emphasise the museum's (or the West's) objectification of cultural artefacts – an analogue for its historical objectification or "othering" of colonial lands.

Exercise

Read the following extracts from Edward Said's book *Orientalism*:

"Every single empire in its official discourse has said that it is not like all the others, that its circumstances are special, that it has a mission to enlighten, civilize, bring order and democracy, and that it uses force only as a last resort. And, sadder still, there always is a chorus of willing intellectuals to say calming words about benign or altruistic empires, as if one shouldn't trust the evidence of one's eyes watching the destruction and the misery and death brought by the latest mission *civilizatrice*."

"The more one is able to leave one's cultural home, the more easily is one able to judge it, and the whole world as well, with the spiritual detachment and generosity necessary for true vision. The more easily, too, does one assess oneself and alien cultures with the same combination of intimacy and distance."

"There is nothing mysterious or natural about authority. It is formed, irradiated, disseminated; it is instrumental, it is persuasive; it has status, it establishes canons of taste and value; it is virtually indistinguishable from certain ideas it dignifies as true, and from traditions, perceptions, and judgments it forms, transmits, reproduces."

How does Khan's 'pot' challenge literary and political *authority*, as characterised by Said? Does the speaker of Mundair's 'Name Journeys' claim some superiority of judgment due to her having left her "cultural home"?

A water pot made out of clay, from Lagos, Nigeria, dates around 1900-1910, Manchester Museum

*Compare how poets present **migration** in 'pot' and one other poem from 'Worlds and lives'.*

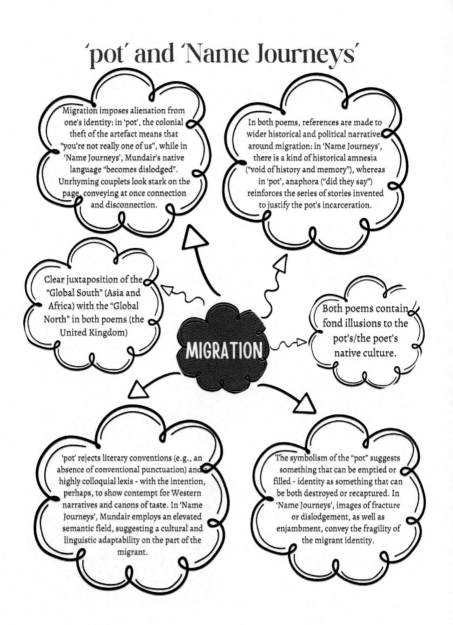

'pot' and 'Name Journeys'

Migration imposes alienation from one's identity: in 'pot', the colonial theft of the artefact means that "you're not really one of us", while in 'Name Journeys', Mundair's native language "becomes dislodged". Unrhyming couplets look stark on the page, conveying at once connection and disconnection.

In both poems, references are made to wider historical and political narrative around migration: in 'Name Journeys', there is a kind of historical amnesia ("void of history and memory"), whereas in 'pot', anaphora ("did they say") reinforces the series of stories invented to justify the pot's incarceration.

Clear juxtaposition of the "Global South" (Asia and Africa) with the "Global North" in both poems (the United Kingdom)

Both poems contain fond illusions to the pot's/the poet's native culture.

MIGRATION

'pot' rejects literary conventions (e.g., an absence of conventional punctuation) and highly colloquial lexis - with the intention, perhaps, to show contempt for Western narratives and canons of taste. In 'Name Journeys', Mundair employs an elevated semantic field, suggesting a cultural and linguistic adaptability on the part of the migrant.

The symbolism of the "pot" suggests something that can be emptied or filled - identity as something that can be both destroyed or recaptured. In 'Name Journeys', images of fracture or dislodgement, as well as enjambment, convey the fragility of the migrant identity.

'A WIDER VIEW', SENI SENEVIRATNE

Contextual background

Seni Seneviratne was raised in Leeds, Yorkshire, and is of English and Sri Lankan heritage.

Seneviratne says that she is "particularly concerned with how to achieve a balance between the public and personal poem; how to find the lyric voice in the face of trauma, violence and catastrophic historical events; how to speak the unspeakable; how to avoid polemic and sentimentality when writing about big issues; how to write in a way that invites empathy; how to change hearts as well as minds through the medium of poetry."

Introduction to the poem

In 'A Wider View', time collapses, transporting the poet from contemporary Leeds to the 19th century's dusty flax mills. The poet imagines the life that her great great grandad must have lived at the height of Victorian industrialisation, along with his rich inner life that was denied expression. A brief moment of "timelessness" is

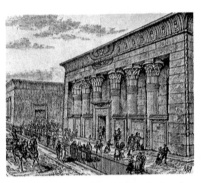

Marshall's flax mill at Holbeck, Leeds, circa 1843

conjured at the poem's close, when the poet and her great great grandad "meet" on the Wharf, connected by the *curve of past and future generations*.

Key thematic features

Industrialisation and the suppression of the self: 'A Wider View' draws upon many of the same themes that concern George Eliot in 'In A London Drawingroom' – industrialisation and the effacement of the individual. However, unlike Eliot's poem, this is not a passive description of the conditions that reduce individuals to anonymous cogs in the capitalist machine, but rather a centering of one human life during one of the greatest upheavals in human history. The poet imagines her great great grandad in his own spiritual struggle against *"the limits of his working life"*, and his desire to see beyond the *"paneled gates of Tower Works"* and hear the *"imagined peals of ringing bells"*.

The importance of place in shaping our identities: There is an abundance of proper nouns in 'A Wider View', bringing emphasis to the landmarks and places that structure our existence and connect us with the past: "Marshall's Temple Mill", "Tower Works", "Harding's chimney", "Neville Street's Dark Arches", the "River Aire" and the "Wharf".

How lives connect across history: The second verse marks a transition away from the specificity of a particular moment in history towards timelessness: *"the red brick vaults begin to moan as time collapsing in the river air sweeps me out to meet him on the wharf. We stand now timeless in the flux of time [...]"* The refocusing on the first-person, the "me" and "we", emphasises that the poem is as much about her granddad as about the reconstruction of her own genealogy – the connecting of lives across history.

Key stylistic features

Powerful imagery: This is a highly empathic poem, filled with powerful images that build a vivid picture of poverty and strife: *"from the backyard of his back to back"*, *"smoke-filled skies"*, *"high enough above the cholera"*, *"eyes dry with dust"*, and *"the din of engines, looms and shuttles"*.

Frequent allusions to place-names: "Marshall's Temple Mill", "Tower Works", "Harding's chimney", "Neville Street's Dark Arches", the "River Aire" and the "Wharf" stand as architectural testaments to the shared history of the poet and her great-great-grandad.

Lexicon of enclosure: Like in Eliot's 'In a London Drawingroom', there is an abundance of lexical items conveying enclosure and entrapment: *"backyard of his back-to-back"*, *"searched for spaces"*, *"smoke-filled sky"*, *"panelled gates"*, and *"the limits of his working life"*.

Figurative, non-literal language, and zeugma: The poem blends several images and ideas into one single grammatical unit, elevating the reader above the literal and preparing us for the blending of time and histories in the poem's second half: *"my great-great-grandad searched for spaces/ in the smoke-filled skies to stack his dreams,/ high enough above the cholera to keep them/ and his newborn safe from harm."* Here, the poet's use of zeugma (*"to keep them and his newborn safe from harm"*) also emphasises the twin dangers that Britain's rapidly-expanding industrialisation and urbanisation pose: threats to spiritual health (or a person's dreams) and threats to physical health (the threat of cholera).

$$\longrightarrow$$

What other poems in the anthology could 'A Wider View' be compared to? What themes do the poems have in common?

- Eliot's 'In a London Drawingroom' - A shared concern with industrialisation and the urban landscape?
- Berry's 'Homing' - A shared interest in how the fabric of history shapes our "now" and our identities?

'HOMING', LIZ BERRY

Contextual background

Liz Berry was born and raised in the Black Country, near Birmingham.

Her works are interleaved with elements of Black Country dialect and vocabulary. The region holds a heavy influence over her poetry, as she explains: "the place haunted me, haunted my work: its darkness, its gutted landscape, its folklore and music, its story of industrial wonder and decline, and – most significantly – its dialect."

Elsewhere, she has said that she wants to "reclaim" the Black Country dialect "as something beautiful to be treasured and celebrated" and use it in "lyric poetry". She describes it as "full of charm and surprise and wonder, but much maligned." "Certainly in a time when accents and areas are becoming more and more similar," Berry says, "I think it is really important to celebrate the differences, the individuality and quirks of speech."

Introduction to the poem

'Homing' is a lament for the lost and deliberately repressed Black Country accent of (we assume) the poet's close relative. Composed of five stanzas of free verse, the poem takes the form of an intimate address of the speaker to her relative, as she clears out their house and remembers their attempt to eradicate difference and emulate a Received Pronunciation accent.

Key thematic features

Identity and heritage: 'Homing' stands as a tribute to the role of language and dialect in determining and shaping identity, as well as its role in preserving regional histories. To the poet, dialects and accents are not mere sounds, but sound-histories that disclose and preserve a way of life: *"the pits,/railways, factories thunking and clanging/the night shift, the red brick/back-to-back you were born in."* In this case, the poet laments the loss of the addressee's Black Country accent, repressed and disguised by *"hours of elocution"* and teachers' reprimands.

Language as a social marker: In this poem, Berry is interested in language as a marker of social class and regional identity. In that standalone image of *"the teacher's ruler across your legs"*, she evokes the brutal means by which these identifiers were flattened and repressed. Her mother's native accent, however, erupts throughout the poem against her best efforts.

Peter Trudgill, author of Peter Trudgill, *Sociolinguistics: An Introduction to Language and Society*:

"The fact is that none of us can unilaterally decide what a word means. Meanings of words are shared between people - they are a kind of social contract we all agree to - otherwise communication would not be possible."

Key stylistic features

Use of dialect words and italicisation: The poet cites the Black Country dialect words, used by her mother, however signals their foreignness in her own mouth by the use of italicisation: *"saft"*, *"blart"*, and *"bibble, fittle, tay, wum"*. Italicisation in the third line of the first and third verses also creates a structural and moral equivalence between the *"how now brown cow"* (or RP English) and the Black Country dialect.

Allusive: The poet says that her *"vowels [were] ferrous as nails, consonants/you could lick the coal from"* – a reference to the Black Country's two major historical industries, ironworking and coal mining. Another allusion is made to the region's historical ironworking industry in the final stanza, when she says: *"I wanted to forge your voice/in my mouth, a blacksmith's furnace."* Like in 'A Wider View', places, landmarks and industries are instrumental in shaping regional and individual identities.

Similes: The poem is replete with suggestive similes and descriptions: she compares her mother's clangorous consonants and vowels to *"nails"* and describes them as *"guttural"* and *"ferrous"*-sounding, and wishes to send her mother's words *"fluttering for home"* *"like pigeons"*.

Second-person address: The poem is written in the second-person, signalling our participation in an intimate address between speaker and addressee.

A positive culminating image: The poem culminates on a jubilant image of *"pigeons,/fluttering for home"*, denoting liberation from the straitjacket of linguistic conventions.

Exercise

Read this extract from Wordsworth's *Preface to Lyrical Ballads*:

"There will also be found in these volumes **little of what is usually called poetic diction**; as much pains has been taken to avoid it as is ordinarily taken to produce it; this has been done for the reason already alleged, to bring my **language near to the language of men** [...]

Aristotle, I have been told, has said, that Poetry is the most philosophic of all writing: it is so: **its object is truth, not individual and local, but general, and operative**; not standing upon external testimony, but carried alive into the heart by passion; truth which is its own testimony, which gives competence and confidence to the tribunal to which it appeals, and receives them from the same tribunal. **Poetry is the image of man and nature.** [...]

The Poet thinks and feels in the spirit of human passions. How, then, can his language differ in any material degree from that of all other men who feel vividly and see clearly? It might be proved that it is impossible. But supposing that this were not the case, the Poet might then be allowed to use a peculiar language when expressing his feelings for his own gratification, or that of men like himself. But Poets do not write for Poets alone, but for men. [...]

Our feelings are the same with respect to metre; for, as it may be proper to remind the Reader, the distinction of metre is regular and uniform, and not, like that which is produced by what is usually called POETIC DICTION, arbitrary, and subject to infinite caprices upon which no calculation whatever can be made. In the one case, the Reader is utterly at the mercy of the Poet, respecting what imagery or diction he may choose to connect with the passion; whereas, in the other, the metre obeys certain laws, to which the Poet and Reader both willingly submit because they are certain, and because no interference is made by them with the passion, but such as the concurring testimony of ages has shown to heighten and improve the pleasure which co-exists with it."

- In what sense, if any, does Berry write in "the language of men"?
- Why does Wordsworth think that it is desirable for a poet to adopt metre?
- What poetic advantages does Berry's enjambment and free verse confer? Easier blending of images? Closer approximation of ordinary prose?

Practice exam question

*Compare how poets present **identity** in 'Homing' and one other poem from 'Worlds and lives'.*

'Homing' and 'Name Journeys'

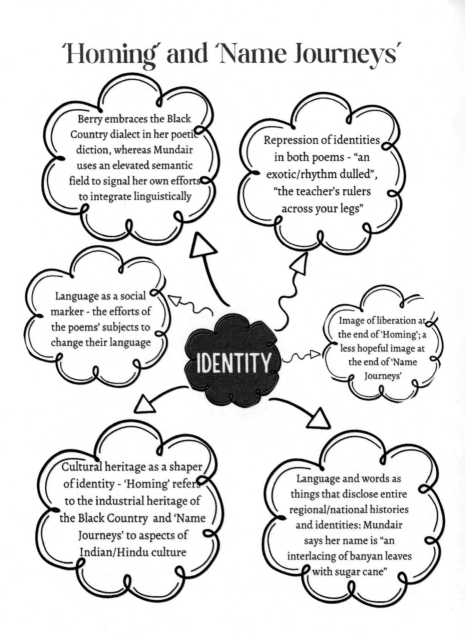

Berry embraces the Black Country dialect in her poetic diction, whereas Mundair uses an elevated semantic field to signal her own efforts to integrate linguistically

Repression of identities in both poems - "an exotic/rhythm dulled", "the teacher's rulers across your legs"

Language as a social marker - the efforts of the poems' subjects to change their language

IDENTITY

Image of liberation at the end of 'Homing'; a less hopeful image at the end of 'Name Journeys'

Cultural heritage as a shaper of identity - 'Homing' refers to the industrial heritage of the Black Country and 'Name Journeys' to aspects of Indian/Hindu culture

Language and words as things that disclose entire regional/national histories and identities: Mundair says her name is "an interlacing of banyan leaves with sugar cane"

'A CENTURY LATER', IMTIAZ DHARKER

Contextual background

Born in Pakistan and raised in Scotland, Imtiaz Dharker is a poet with bases in both London and India. Her diverse heritage and itinerant existence forms the essence of her writing: her poetry traverses themes of geographical and cultural displacement, conflict, and gender politics, while interrogating received ideas about home, freedom, and faith.

Introduction to the poem

Shortlisted for the 2014 Ted Hughes Award, Dharker wrote 'A Century Later' 100 years after the outbreak of the First World War as a response to Wilfred Owen's 'Anthem for Doomed Youth'. The poem places iconic imagery of the war (*"a field humming under the sun,/its lap open and full of poppies"*, *"take their places on the frontline"*) in a contemporary context, drawing parallels between the plight of the young male combatants in the trenches and the plight of women fighting for an education. Echoes of Owen's poem resound throughout 'A Century Later'.

The poem also makes reference to the shooting of Malala Yousafzai in Swat, Pakistan in 2012: *"The missile cuts a pathway in her mind"*. Yousafzai became the target of an unsuccessful assassination attempt at the hands of the Pakistani Taliban after campaigning for girls' right to an education.

Key thematic features

Defiance in the face of injustice: Owen's 'Anthem for Doomed Youth' is in no way consolatory, but rather poetically rehearse the stark facts of modern industrialised warfare. Unlike the traditional elegy, it does not participate in the nationalist ideology of compensation that would have remembrance stand in as repayment for loss of life. It instead bewails the animal, anonymous and unheroic deaths of *"these who die as cattle"*. 'A Century Later', by contrast, takes a more defiant tone, celebrating the unchecked power of the human spirit: *"Behind her, one by one,/the schoolgirls are standing up/to take their places on the front line."* In the penultimate verse, Yousafzai is given a voice and she says, in the declarative second-person: *"Bullet, she says, you are stupid./You have failed. You cannot kill a book/or the buzzing in it."*

The power of the word: Yousafzai gained prominence by using her voice to campaign for women's rights and freedoms. 'A Century Later' celebrates this power of words to transform minds, recasting the famous metonymic adage, "The pen is mightier than the sword", in that memorable line: *"You cannot kill a book/or the buzzing in it."* Violence, paradoxically, becomes a catalyst for non-violent action, uniting all schoolgirls in the fight for educational parity with men.

The fight for women's rights:
Dharker emphasises that Yousafzai's aims are not particularly lofty by listing quotidian experiences – she is campaigning for the *"right to be ordinary"* or the right to enjoy the simple joys of life: reading a book, going to school, wearing bangles to a wedding, painting fingernails.

Key stylistic features

Intertextual and allusive: 'A Century Later' exhibits intertextuality – that is, it shapes its own meaning via references to other texts. It explicitly alludes to Owen's 'Anthem for Doomed Youth', most notably in its opening line: "*The school-bell is a call to battle*". Owen's poem similarly opens with a reference to bells in the rhetorical question: "*What passing-bells for these who die as cattle?*" 'A Century Later' also features the widely-recognised symbolism of poppies which flourished in churned soil of the Western Front. In drawing upon other texts and culturally-loaded symbols, Dharker's poem summons up a whole network of meanings, assimilating the fight for women's education into the same monumental arc of history that encompasses the world's major conflicts.

Metaphor: The image of a "missile" cutting its way through the air is unexpectedly confounded by imagery of trees, of blooming wildlife. Rather than presenting scenes of bloodshed and terror, Yousafzai's mind is compared "*to an orchard/in full bloom, a field humming under the sun,/its lap open and full of poppies*", denoting mental freedom and creativity – something unharmed by the machinery of war.

Structural features: Frequent enjambment is used to bring emphasis to certain ideas. In the second stanza, enjambment brings added surprise to that sentence ending, "*and walks on*", as the Taliban's attempts to stifle women are thwarted. Enjambment also creates an element of surprise in the fourth stanza. "*The girl has won*" prepares us for some glorious reward, however the reward is merely "*the right to be ordinary*".

What other poems in the anthology could 'A Century Later' be compared to?

- Shelley's 'England in 1819'? A shared interest in social and political injustice?

Exercise

Read this extract from Malala Yousafzai's Nobel Lecture, delivered in 2014:

"Dear brothers and sisters, I was named after the inspirational Malalai of Maiwand who is the Pashtun Joan of Arc. The word Malala means "grief stricken," "sad," but in order to lend some happiness to it, my grandfather would always call me "Malala —The happiest girl in the world" and today I am very happy that we are together fighting for an important cause. [...]

I have found that people describe me in many different ways. Some people call me the girl who was shot by the Taliban. And some, the girl who fought for her rights. Some people call me a "Nobel Laureate" now. However, my brothers still call me that annoying bossy sister. As far as I know, I am just a committed and even stubborn person who wants to see every child getting quality education, who wants to see women having equal rights and who wants peace in every corner of the world.

Education is one of the blessings of life—and one of its necessities. That has been my experience during the 17 years of my life. In my paradise home, Swat, I always loved learning and discovering new things. I remember when my friends and I would decorate our hands with henna on special occasions. And instead of drawing flowers and patterns we would paint our hands with mathematical formulas and equations. We had a thirst for education, because our future was right there in that classroom. We would sit and learn and read together. We loved to wear neat and tidy school uniforms and we would sit there with big dreams in our eyes. We wanted to make our parents proud and prove that we could also excel in our studies and achieve those goals, which some people think only boys can."

Contextual background

Raymond Antrobus was born in Hackney, London, to an English mother and Jamaican father. He was born deaf, however seven years passed before he was diagnosed.

This straddling of two worlds – a world where sound is taken for granted and a world of silence – is explored in his debut collection, *The Perserverence.*

He is the recipient of many awards and in 2019, he became the first poet to win the Rathbone Folio Prize for the best new work of literature published in the English language that year. He has an MBE for services to literature, and has an MA in Spoken Word Education from Goldsmiths University. Most recently, he has been shortlisted for the T.S. Eliot prize 2021.

Introduction to the poem

The poem, written largely in unrhymed couplets, explores man's complex relationship with nature, as we find ourselves both alienated from it and emotionally, spiritually dependent on it. 'With Birds You're Never Lonely' is highly sensorial, with vibrant visual imagery as well as a soundscape of urban and earthly sounds. The poem may seem (consciously or unconsciously) to draw upon a long intellectual tradition, beginning in the

18th century Enlightenment, of seeing in Polynesia a model of harmonious human life. It might also be characterised as ecopoetry insofar as it concerns the natural non-human world, and is ecocentric rather than anthropocentric, placing special emphasis on nature's needs.

Key thematic features

Our relationship with nature and our role on the planet: In opening two couplets, the poem immediately locates us within an urban landscape: "*I can't hear the barista/over the coffee machine./Spoons slam, steam rises. [...]*" This mundane event is then juxtaposed with the exotic Polynesian landscape – the "*Zelandia forest/with sun-syrupped Kauri trees/and brazen Tui birds with white tufts/and yellow and black beaks.*" There, the natives have been bequeathed a knowledge and love of the natural world. A young Maori woman is described as knowing which songs belong to which birds, and repeats her grandfather's phrase: "*with birds you're never lonely.*" The young Maori woman, whose knowledge of the natural world is inherited and almost visceral, also contrasts with the man reading in the cafe, whose knowledge of the natural world is purely academic, being derived from books.

The sharp transition from the Zelandia forest back to London with its "*grey tree*[s]" underscores urban populations' alienation from the natural world and the spiritual poverty of places divorced from nature. Transitioning abruptly from description to philosophical contemplation, the poet rhetorically asks "*what the trees would say about us?/What books would they write if they had to cut us down?*" – foregrounding nature's needs. The poem ends by personifying London's trees, as the poet regrets "*the family they don't have,/the Gods they can't hold.*"

Silence, sound and communication: The poem is about, quite literally, the difficult of "tuning" into nature, as the speaker wrestles with his hearing aids to let in the right amount of sound. A semantic field of sound and noise is prominent in the poem: "*can't hear*", "*slam*", *blaring so loudly*", "*all sound disappeared*", "*a silence*", "*silence collapsed*", "*listened*", "*chirped*". However, silence – so foreign to the modern world – is "*not an absence*", the poet says.

Key stylistic features

Structural features: 'With Birds You're Never Lonely' is organised into 17 couplets and a single standalone line at the end. The couplets might suggest balance, harmony and simplicity, while the standalone line might serve to unseat this harmony, implying alienation and disharmony. The further implication might be that man's relationship with nature is now "out of joint". The lines describing the urban scene are also notably shorter than those describing the Zelandia forest, suggesting a different pace of life.

Juxtaposition: There are a number of juxtapositions throughout the poem – between the urban and the rural, the mundane and the exotic, sound and silence – which may serve to illustrate how far removed we are from the natural world.

Sensorial language: The poem conveys the meditative state of the poet, as he becomes immersed in the varied sights and sounds of both a London café and the Zelandia forest in New Zealand. He conjures up this sensory experience with highly evocative language: *"Spoons slam, steam rises"*, *"sun-syrupped Kauri trees"*, *"brazen Tui birds with white tufts/and yellow and black beaks"*, *"blaring"*, *"silence collapsed"*, and *"the earthy Kauri trees, their endless/brown and green trunks of sturdiness"*.

Exercise

Read the following John Shoptaw's analysis of the genre of *ecopoetry*:

"What is ecopoetry? What must an ecopoem be to do justice to its name? My answer is twofold: an ecopoem needs to be environmental and it needs to be environmentalist. By environmental, I mean first that an ecopoem needs to be about the nonhuman natural world — wholly or partly, in some way or other, but really and not just figuratively. In other words, an ecopoem is a kind of nature poem. But an ecopoem needs more than the vocabulary of nature. [...]

An ecopoem is environmentalist not only thematically, in that it represents environmental damage or risk, but rhetorically: it is urgent, it aims to unsettle. But doesn't environmentalist poetry then risk complacency at least as much as nature poetry? Aren't ecopoets deluding themselves into thinking that their poems can change anything? "For poetry," as Auden declared in his elegy "In Memory of W.B. Yeats," "makes nothing happen." Auden's proposition, though, is not a fact but a belief. A similar skepticism today informs discussions about efficacy and causality. [...]

The more immediate hazard for ecopoetry, then, is didacticism. If a contemporary nature poem risks being immoral, an ecopoem, whatever its effects, risks being moralistic. How can an ecopoem usher us into a new environmental imagination without teaching us a tiresome lesson? In light of the prevailing tendency to value poetic form over (natural) content, it may be instructive to summarize the history of aestheticism, from which this tendency derives. Kant's non-teleological, purely formal "purposiveness without purpose" passes into romanticism ("Beauty is truth, truth beauty") and the aesthetic movement ("art for art's sake") [...]"

Credit: 'Why Ecopoetry?', John Shoptaw from *Poetry Magazine*

In what sense (if any) are 'With Birds You're Never Lonely' and 'Like an Heiress' examples of "ecopoetry"? Do either of the poems "unsettle" the reader? Are they didactic, or do they content themselves with a "purposiveness without purpose"?

'A PORTABLE PARADISE', ROGER ROBINSON

Contextual background

Roger Robinson is a black writer and performer who splits his time between Londo and Trinidad in the Caribbean. 'A Portable Paradise' is the titular poem of his collection *A Portable Paradise*, published in 2019.

One critic writes that his "work is shrouded in darkness, a tenebrous blanket that provokes our every sense." "From quotidian calamities and injustice, to the recount of history's darkest hours," they say, "Robinson relentlessly reminds us of the evil that stalks the land. Suffering is ubiquitous, shadowing our every move."

Introduction to the poem

Robinson says that 'A Portable Paradise' "originates in my experience of returning to England from Trinidad when I was 19. Before I left Trinidad, there was a popular song by an Australian band called Crowded House. The chorus went 'Everywhere you go always take the weather with you'. When faced with my first winter (when winter was really winter) I'd find myself singing that song to try and cheer up, as my left my Grandmother's house to go to my industrial laundry job. The work was arduous and I found myself constantly looking at pictures from Trinidad."

Written in free verse, the poem is a celebration of the power of imagination, and is built around a single piece of advice given to the poet by his grandmother. It represents the poet's personal vision of "Paradise", which for Robinson resembles the "white sands, green hills and fresh fish" of tropical Trinidad.

Key thematic features

Imagination as a form of escapism and resilience: Robinson positions himself as a *poète engagé* (a politically engaged poet) in many of his works, having written about prominent socio-political issues such as the Grenfell disaster, Windrush, slavery, the Brixton riots and the death of Rashan Charles. In 'A Portable Paradise', however, he creates an imaginative space away from these oppressive social realities, conjuring up his own personal vision of paradise. For the poet, paradise is a representation of the Caribbean, with its *"white sands, green hills and fresh fish"*. One critic says that paradise is used as "a potent symbol for psychic resilience", offering a tool to live alongside an unjust social order.

Family and an inheritance of fortitude: The source of the poem's wisdom is the poet's grandmother, testifying (like Kipling's poem 'If') to the family's role in bequeathing fortitude, heritage and resilience: *"And if I speak of Paradise/then I'm speaking of my grandmother."*

Key stylistic features

Echoes of Kipling's 'If' and anaphora: We might hear echoes of Rudyard Kipling's famous poem, 'If', which similarly endorses a powerful vision of stoicism and which similarly uses anaphora (the repetition of the word 'If') to create rhetorical emphasis. Unlike Kipling's 'If', however, 'A Portable Paradise' does not provide guidance on how the reader should interact with the external world, but rather endorses introspection and internal retreat.

Extended metaphor: The poem uses the extended metaphor of a physical object to illustrate how people should relate to their personal paradises. A paradise, like a physical object, can be stolen, it can be held in the pocket, it can be smelt and felt, and it can be emptied onto a desk. In this way, the poet represents the alchemical power of imagination, its ability to transform pure figments into the stuff of reality.

Imagery of hope: The poem ends on an image of hope and renewal: *"Shine the lamp on it like the fresh hope/or morning, and keep starting at it till you sleep."*

Loose, conversational effect: The poem's extensive use of caesura and enjambment contributes to its loose, conversational effect, drawing the reader into a confidence that feels intimate and unstudied.

'LIKE AN HEIRESS', GRACE NICHOLS

Contextual background

Nichols, born in 1950 in Guyana, moved to the United Kingdom in 1977. Her works draw inspiration from the rich tapestry of her homeland's history and culture, in particular its oral storytelling tradition, its history of enslavement, it landscapeand its folk tales.

Upon arrival in the UK, Nichols' work began to address contemporary socio-political issues. Alongside Kwesi-Johnson and Agard, who were also part of the West-Indian poet community, Nichols' work explored racial tensions at a time when immigration was a focal point of political discourse under Margaret Thatcher's government.

There is, however, often an emphasis on universality and cultural commonality in her works. In her poem, 'Hurricane Hits England', the extreme weather reminds her that "the earth is the earth is the earth."

Introduction to the poem

'Like an Heiress' joins Antrobus' 'With Birds You're Never Lonely' as an example of "ecopoetry" – nature poetry that prompts the reader to examine their relationship to the world and how they act and live in it. In this case, the poem, a recollection of a visit to a beach on the Atlantic coast, takes aim at the vast quantities of human-generated waste suffocating the world's oceans.

Key thematic features

Identity and heritage: 'Like an Heiress' narrates the poet's return to her country of birth, and the unexpected, jarring sense of foreignness, heralded by the connective "*But*". She hopes to recapture her "*oceanic small-days*", but instead she is met by an empty beach. Later, she returns "*like a tourist/to the sanctuary of [her] hotel room*", with the telling simile suggesting that Guyana no longer feels like home.

Ecological crisis: Nichols also dwells on the ecological crisis that has began to engulf her country of birth. She speaks of a "*lone/wave of rubbish against the old seawall,/used car tyres, plastic bottles, styrofoam cups,*" and mother nature's antipathy to the assault on her integrity. To represent this, Nichols personifies the ocean: "*rightly tossed back by an ocean's moodswings*". Guyana's approach to waste disposal, like that of many other emerging economies, is characterised by a great deal of illegal dumping on open streets, alleyways and waterways. Nichols, however, does not exempt herself as a causal factor in environmental degradation: at the end of the poem, she "*[dwells] in the air-conditioned coolness*" of her hotel room. Air conditioning generates about four percent of global greenhouse gas emissions – twice as much as the aviation industry. There is a sense of philosophical resignation and fatalism at the end of the poem, as she thinks about "*the quickening years and fate of our planet.*"

Key stylistic features

Sonnet form: The poem takes a sonnet form – possibly serving as a homage to Nichols' adopted English culture. However, the traditional iambic pentameter quickly gives way to free verse, signalling perhaps a return or recapture of her native culture.

Lexicon of wealth: The futility of the poet's newfound wealth seems to be underscored by the clash between the lexicon of affluence (*heiress, jewels*) and the imagery of discarded waste ("*wave of rubbish*").

Allusions to Guyanese culture: Nichols is drawn "*to the mirror of [her] oceanic small-days*" – which is possibly an allusion to "Small Days", a traditional Guyanese folk song about nostalgia for childhood.

Personification: Nichols personifies inanimate aspects of nature ("an ocean's moodswings"), perhaps in an attempt to close this chasm between man and nature.

Asyndeton: The poem uses asyndeton (that is, the deliberate omission of conjunctions) in order to convey the undifferentiated tidal wave of rubbish affecting Guyana's shores: "*used car tyres, plastic bottles, styrofoam cups*".

What other poems in the anthology could 'Like an Heiress' be compared to?

- Shamshad Khan's 'pot'? How do Khan and Nichols differ in how they represent the experience of returning to one's native country?
- Antrobus' 'With Birds You're Never Lonely'? How do they represent man's relationship with nature and the reality of anthropogenic ecological destruction?

Compare how poets present **man's relationship with nature** in 'With Birds You're Never Lonely' and one other poem from 'Worlds and Lives'.

'Like an Heiress' and 'With Birds You're Never Lonely'

Both poems contain elements of irony - in Antrobus' poem, a man reads a book about trees in a city where trees are cut down, and in Nichols' poem, the poet retreats to an air-conditioned room, which is in turn exacerbating global warming - or the "sun's burning treasury".

In 'Like an Heiress', nature takes on a threatening aspect ("the sun's burning treasury", "an ocean's moodswings") from which the poet must take refuge: she returns to the "sanctuary" of her hotel room. 'With Birds You're Never Lonely' ends, by contrast, on an expression of pity for nature: "In that moment I felt sorry..."

Both poems engage in the personification of nature, humanising something that has become a mere means to an end: "an ocean's moodswings" and "I wondered what the trees/would say about us?"

MAN'S RELATIONSHIP WITH NATURE

Both poems move from observations to more abstract philosophical contemplation about the fate of the planet.

Both poems engage in juxtaposition - of the manmade and the natural - illustrating how far removed we have become from the natural world. Fittingly, 'With Birds You're Never Lonely' ends on a single standalone line, isolated from the preceding couplets - a final structural comment on man's isolation from nature.

Both poems might be said to belong to the broader subgenre of "ecopoetry" insofar as they not only represent environmental risk thematically, but also *rhetorically*; they aim to unsettle the reader with their urgency.

'THIRTEEN', CALEB FEMI

Contextual background

Born in 1990, Caleb Femi is a British-Nigerian writer, film-maker and photographer. He became London's first young people's laureate in 2016.

His first collection, 'Poor', was described by one critic as "poetic journalism" and is interleaved with his own original photography. This, he explains, is because his poems and artistic works carry with them a sense of "archival responsibility" – that is, they hope to register real stories and experiences not shaped by the media.

In the collection, he muses on systemic racism, classism, police brutality and gentrification, while experimenting with hip-hop, fragmentation, image and modern lyric.

Introduction to the poem

Femi's 'Thirteen' bears some resemblances to the poetic genre of confessionalism, narrating the poet's experience of racial profiling by a police officer at the tender age of thirteen. It describes the abrupt loss of innocence (*"fear condenses on your lips"*) as the boy tries and fails to summon up a shared moment in time and create rapport: *"Don't you remember me? You will ask./You gave a talk at my primary school."* The poem's close figuratively describes this loss of innocence through the imagery of a dying star – a supernova.

Key thematic features

Racial discrimination: The first line of the poem creates an impending sense of danger, implying that his journey home will not be without obstacles (*"You will be four minutes from home/when* [...]), while the vagueness of the officer's language (*"You fit/the description of a man?"*) tells us that this is not a well-evidenced apprehension of a suspect, but an absurd case of racial profiling and discrimination. In the second verse, the young Femi is excluded from the language of aspiration that his white peers receive. The policeman's glib words (*"he told your class that/you were all supernovas,/the biggest and brightest stars."*), it transpires, were only intended for the white subsection of his school. In the third verse, as the young boy recognises the futility of reasoning with the officers, the poet offers a sinister and fatalistic metaphor for their predatory behaviour: *"You will watch the two men cast lots for your organs."*

Key stylistic features

Direct, colloquial speech rhythms: 'Thirteen' is written in direct, colloquial speech rhythms, giving it an unstudied, unmediated effect. Note, too, the use of the word *"fed"* – British slang for "police officer". This colloquialism brings the reader more fully into the world of Caleb Femi – a North Peckham estate in London.

Extended metaphor: The poet uses the extended metaphor of stars and dying stars (supernovas) to represent the chasm between the aspirations and promise of white children and those of their black counterparts. The metaphor, which is a symbol of unrealised potential in the second verse, metastasizes into a more bleak symbol by the final verse: supernovas, these impossibly bright stars, *"are, in fact, dying stars/on the verge of becoming black holes."*

Uneven stanzas with irregular metre: Uneven stanzas and irregular metre again contributes to the poem's colloquialism, and registers the boy's shifting, ever-changing cognizance of the situation – from laughing disbelief (*"You'll laugh."*) to fear.

Second-person and future-tense narration: The use of the second-person might signify a number of different things. It might serve to make the reader a proxy for the poet, enabling him/her to live the poet's experience more fully. The combination of the second-person and future-tense narration might also suggest that this is the poet's address to his younger self – a cautionary tale and an extension of compassion towards the thirteen year old boy of his past. One critic describes Femi's collection as representing "poetry as incantation and a coping mechanism" – as a way, perhaps, of coming to terms with past trauma.

What other poems in the anthology could 'Thirteen' be compared to?

- Shamshad Khan's 'pot'? Both of them work to explode racial stereotypes by giving centre-stage to the stories of the marginalised.
- James Berry's 'On an Afternoon Train from Purley to Victoria, 1955'? Both Berry and Femi see the humorous absurdity of racism: while the thirteen year-old boy in 'Thirteen' laughs with incredulity when asked whether he fits "the description of a man", the speaker in Berry's poem finds a way to distill humour from his interaction with the Quaker.

Contextual background

Louisa Adjoa Parker is a writer and poet of Ghanaian and English heritage who lives in south-west England. Her works focus on social issues such as rural racism, black history, and mental health.

Introduction to the poem

The visually- and sensorially-striking poem is an exploration of a time-honoured and family tradition of jewellery making – a craft that the man (the poet's father?) in the poem takes pride in. In the final stanza, the poet hints at the economic gulf between his own living conditions and those of the jewellery-wearers – a fleeting and subtle allusion to the marginalisation of manual labourers.

Here, we might hear echoes of Seni Seneviratne's 'A Wider View', which engages in a similar "bringing to life" of the poet's familial heritage of manual marginalised work.

What does jewellery represent and why do people wear it?
- A status symbol?

What does it suggest about the wearer?
- Wealth?
- A non-manual white-collar worker?

Key thematic features

Heritage: The identity of the man remains unknown, however there are clues which imply the Ghanaian heritage of the poet: the walk to the workshop is accompanied by *"the slap of sandaled feet on heat-baked stone"* and takes place under a *"plate blue sky"*, while his wife's skin is described as *"wrinkled by sun"*. Further, the poet says that this career has been followed by the man's father *"and his father too"*, and has taken on an element of eternality: the poem is written in the present tense and uses the adverbial phrase, *"each day"*. Seneviratne also achieves this element of eternality when discussing heritage, representing herself and her great great grandad standing *"timeless in the flux of time"*.

Marginalisation: In the final stanza, the poet subtly evokes the chasm that exists between the jewellery maker and those *"bird-boned"* women who wear his jewellery. While his wife wears a *"simple cotton dress"* and only a *"plain gold band"* that has "worn thin" as jewelley, the wearers of his jewellery enjoy highly-particularised and imaginative creations of *"fine-spun gold"*. There is also the juxtaposition between his wife's time-worn wrinkled face, and the *"clear-eyed, bird-boned, unlined skin"* of the women who will wear his jewellery. Although the man is represented as enjoying his craft ("He *likes hot metal, the smell, the way it yields to his touch"* and "He *likes the tiny loops and curls"*), one feels the injustice of a man unable to enjoy proper remuneration for his *"deft"* labour. At the poem's end, the jewellery maker imagines an intangible human connection between himself and the women whose skin will *"[warm] the metal his hands caress."*

Key stylistic features

Enjambment and caesura enforced by semi-colons: Carefully-placed enjambment and caesura forces the reader to linger over each the man's creations: *"Under the deft fingers gold butterflies dance;/flowers bloom; silvery moons wax and wane,/then wax again; bright dragonflies flap two pairs of wins."* The reader will note the contrast between the ornateness of the jewellery and the man's simple, humble existence.

Sensuous, highly-sensorial descriptions: The poem vividly represents the jewellery maker's world by taking us inside his sensory world with a concentration of highly sense-focussed descriptions: *"in the distance, a wild dog barks"*, *"The smell of blossom"*, *"the slap of sandalled feet"*, *"the smell [of hot metal], the way it yields to his touch"*.

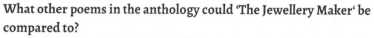

What other poems in the anthology could 'The Jewellery Maker' be compared to?

- Seni Seneviratne's 'A Wider View'? A shared interest in familial history? A "bringing to life" of this heritage?
- While Seneviratne's sensory language conveys the oppressive conditions Victorian industrialisation (*"eyes dry with dust"*, *"din of engines, looms and shuttles"*), Parker's sensory choices might seem to paint a more romanticised view of deprivation.

Model comparative analysis

Example: *Compare how poets present heritage in 'The Jewellery Maker' and one other poem from 'Worlds and Lives'.*

Both Adjoa Parker's 'The Jewellery Maker' and Seneviratne's 'A Wider View' are concerned with **familial heritage** and recount the stories of marginalised male figures through **dense sensorial descriptions**. In 'The Jewellery Maker', the identity of the man remains unknown, however there are clues which imply the Ghanaian heritage of the poet: the walk to the workshop is accompanied by *"the slap of sandaled feet on heat-baked stone"* and takes place under a *"plate blue sky"*, while his wife's skin is described as *"wrinkled by sun"*. Further, the poet says that this career has been passed down the generations (*"like his father before him and his father too"*), suggesting an element of eternality or fatalism. The poem is also written in the **present tense** and uses the **adverbial phrase**, *"each day"*, while Seneviratne also suggests the eternality and indelible character of heritage, with the **past tense** of the poem's first-half transitioning seamlessly into the **present tense** in the second half, where she describes herself and her great great granddad standing *"timeless in the flux of time"*. The two family members become connected even across the great gulf of time.

However, unlike 'The Jewellery Maker', 'A Wider View' is also concerned with **national, as well as familial, heritage** — namely, **the heritage of the industrial revolution**, with its lasting monuments of mechanisation and production (the 'Wharf', the chimneys, mills, and back-to-back terrace houses) that linger on into the present day. The **importance of place in grounding heritage** is reflected through an abundance of **proper nouns and place names**. 'The Jewellery Maker', by contrast, is less concerned with the grand sweep of history than the **social stratification** that appears to have been passed down the generations — manifested by social markers such as simple jewellery, simple dress, and time-worn wrinkled skin. Moreover, while Seneviratne's **sensory language** conveys the oppressive conditions of Victorian industrialisation ("eyes dry with dust", "din of engines, looms and shuttles"), Parker's sensory choices might seem to paint a more **romanticised view** of inherited deprivation.

Writing an introduction

There is no set formula for writing an introduction, however a good approach is to briefly outline how your comparative poetry analysis is going to unfold. For example, you might want to give a brief introduction to the two poems that you are going to analyse, before demarcating their main points of similarity and difference. This will not only show the examiner that you intend to carry out a sustained comparison, but it will also function as a helpful "roadmap" for you when writing your essay.

Example: *Compare how poets present the migrant experience in 'Name Journeys' and one other poem from 'Worlds and lives'.*

Introduction: "Raman Mundair's 'Name Journeys' is a highly figurative exploration of the migrant's dislocating experience of moving to Britain, a place where the cultural way-markers that would make sense of her name and identity are notably absent. James Berry's 'On an Afternoon Train From Purley to Victoria, 1955' explores a similar theme, as the speaker and the well-intentioned Quaker talk at cross purposes about origins and racial brotherhood. The central conflict, in both cases, arises from Britain's historical amnesia, as the speakers' interlocutors fail to grasp the full import of Britain's colonial history. However, while Berry's poem ends on a hopeful image of understanding, Mundair's poem ends on a note of cynicism, condemning her adopted culture as "the Anglo echo chamber, void of history and memory."

The "meat"

There are different ways to structure your essay, however an effective way might be to explore two similarities between your chosen poems across two paragraphs and two differences across another two paragraphs. Within these paragraphs, you may wish to adopt the PEEL (Point, Example/Evidence, Explanation and Link to the next paragraph) technique, to ensure that you are providing a thorough response that covers the assessment objectives. Always remember the importance of literary, historical or cultural context for framing or supplementing your response!

Example: *Compare how poets present* **clashes between worlds** *in 'Thirteen' and one other poem from 'Worlds and lives'.*

Both Femi's 'Thirteen' and Dharker's 'A Century Later' present clashes between two distinct political worlds. In the latter, the hopeful, liberal worldview of Malala Yousafzai, who wishes for nothing more than the "right to be ordinary", collides with the murderous illiberalism of the Taliban. In the former, the young Femi's innocence collides with institutional racism — in an era characterised by the murder of Stephen Lawrence and the over-policing of black communities. In 'A Century Later', this clash is represented by the surprising juxtaposition of violent imagery ("The missile cuts/a pathway to her mind") and imagery symbolically representing life, freedom, potential and creativity ("to an orchard/in full bloom, a field humming under the sun/ its lap open and full of poppies", etc.). Here, Yousafzai's world of freedom emerges triumphant, heralded by that standalone couplet: "This girl has won/ the right to be ordinary". In 'Thirteen', the clash is represented in the metastasization of the "supernova" extended metaphor from a symbol of hope and unrealised potential into a symbol of self-destruction and emptiness: supernovas "are, in fact, dying stars/on the verge of becoming black holes." Unlike in 'A Century Later', the young Femi does not emerge triumphant over his pursuers, and the poem is weighed down by fatalistic metaphors, such as that of the officers casting lots for his organs, before ending on the image of a black hole. However, while Dharker frames the clash between two conflictual worlds as part of the great monumental arc of history that also encompasses the world wars, Femi is more concerned with how individual subjectivities encounter institutional racism.

Writing a conclusion

A conclusion only needs to be short and should briefly summarize what you have established in the course of your essay. You may wish to summarize the core similarity and the core difference between the two poems' approach to the theme.

Complete grade 9 model comparative poetry essay

*Compare how poets present **a sense of dissatisfaction with the world** in 'England in 1819' and one other poem from 'Worlds and lives'.*

Shelley's 'England in 1819' and Wordsworth's 'Lines Written in Early Spring' both conform to **Romanticism's championing of personal ideals and shunning of society's conventions and strictures**, seeing in the latter the source of man's woes and dissatisfaction. Reacting to the horrors of the Peterloo Massacre in Manchester, Shelley's 'England in 1819' weaponises one of poetry's most enduring structures, the **sonnet**, in order to paint a sweeping mural of England's corrupt institutions. Defying audience expectations, the sonnet will culminate with cautious optimism on **an image of revolutionary hope**. By contrast, 'Lines Written in Early Spring' takes a more metaphysical or philosophical approach to man's dissatisfaction, seeing in the sublimity of nature a panacea to man's ills.

British Romanticism was marked, not only by an aesthetic revolution, but also by an accompanying period of societal and political upheaval that was defined by the Industrial Revolution, the rise of liberalism, and the free expression of radical ideas. In the **political sonnet** 'England in 1819', these radical anti-monarchical ideas find explicit expression as the speaker rails against the England's institutional corruption. The **one-sentence structure with its stack of subject clauses** gives the sense of an unchecked, almost breathless anger that will build until the poem's hopeful climax in the final two lines. The **plosive alliteration** of "blind in blood, without a blow", and the **sibilant alliteration** of "A people starv'd and stabb'd", provides further emphasis to each element in this litany of wrongs. Wordsworth's 'Lines Written in Early Spring', by contrast, takes a less political, and more metaphysical approach to man's dissatisfaction with the world, exploring a breach in man's "link" to Nature.

Wordsworth's poetic works frequently espouse a belief in an "*anima mundi*" — or a psyche of the universe which is the source of all being. This peculiar system of thought asserted that the same spirit that animates nature is present in man as well. However, in 'Lines Written in Early Spring', it is man's deviation from the purifying, restorative power of nature that preoccupies him. After emphasising the "link" between "Nature" and the "human soul" ("To her fair works did Nature link/The human soul that through me ran"), Wordsworth introduces **a jarring note of dissonance** as he recognises that humankind has rejected the spiritual interdependence between man and nature. The **iambic trimeter** in the final line of each stanza unseats the posited harmony between man and nature, creating a **"rhythmic as well as semantic sense of something missing"** (A. Potkay). It is never clear exactly "what man has made of man", this being left (deliberately?) unspecified, however Wordsworth's contemporary reader might have thought of **the ongoing revolutionary events in France**, where regime change and the bloody Napoleonic wars were the order of the day. Löwy and Sayre note that **the French Revolution was an ambiguous historical development for the Romantics**: on the one hand, it was the culmination of a fantastic idealism, and on the other, it represented a consolidation by the bourgeois class of its growing economic hegemony. For Wordsworth, initial enthusiasm would transmute into rejection.

Shelley, however, identified more fervently with the Revolution of 1789, including with its more radical outcroppings, and 'England in 1819' is structured in such a way as to demonstrate antiquated political systems' role as the wellspring of political injustice and man's dissatisfaction with the world. The list of England's ills begins with **an allusive description** of George III as the "old, mad, blind, despis'd and dying King", whose Hanoverian bloodline pollutes everything that it touches "like mud from a muddy spring". These **thundering "d" sounds** and the **hostile caricatures** of England's elite conveys the pent-up disdain of a betrayed people, while astute readers might be reminded of Shakespeare's depiction of the mad King Lear. Deliberate vagueness, or **semantic ambiguity**, in the poem's terms of reference ("A people starved and stabbed in th' untilled field") widens the group of people against whom these crimes have been committed: the "field" could refer to St Peter's or any field left untilled by **the Corn Laws**.

The poem, however, will be topped by **a cautiously optimistic finale**, positing a possible release from England's corruption: "Are graves from which a glorious Phantom may/ Burst, to illumine our tempestuous day." Cautious, because the poem hinges on that **modal verb "may"** and the form of this victory ("a glorious Phantom") remains phantasmal. Man's link to Nature also seems tenuously held in 'Lines Written in Early Spring', where the speaker's identification with Nature's anima seems undermined by his own **uncertain discourse**. The poem opens, for example, on the line, "I heard a thousand blended notes," implying a confusion of voices. It is also interleaved with various **tentative constructions**: "I must think, do all I can", "It seemed", and "And 'tis my faith". In both cases, then, the poems' utopianism might seem to occupy an ambiguous status, never quite achieving full-fledged expression — as one failed revolution teeters on the edge of another.

To conclude, both 'Lines Written in Early Spring' and 'England in 1819' identify man-made culture as the source of man's dissatisfaction. In the former, the easy play of Nature, shot-through with a divine animism, highlights the severe lack or absence affecting man, however this absence is never quite resolved, leaving us with a structural and semantic sense of something missing. In the latter, Revolution remains phantasmal, a mere possibility or modality that must face down a corruption that is both congenital ("the dregs of their dull race") and institutional.

Grade 9 elements of this response:

- Early use of contextual information draws out a point of comparison
- Judicious use of subject terminology, used to support interpretations of meaning
- Both poems explored in parallel, using an analysis of one to illuminate the other
- Original approach to the poems that goes beyond GCSE-level analysis, drawing upon critics' comments,
- Poised modal verbs used to show openness to other interpretations: "could refer", "seems undermined", "implying", "might seem to occupy", etc.

Compare how poets present **a sense of dissatisfaction with the world** in 'England in 1819' and one other poem from 'Worlds and lives'.

Compare how poets present **the shaping of lives by social and political conditions** in 'In a London Drawingroom' and one other poem from 'Worlds and lives'.

Compare how poets present **the migrant experience** in 'Name Journeys' and one other poem from 'Worlds and lives'.

Compare how poets present **emigration to new worlds** in 'pot' and one other poem from 'Worlds and lives'.

Compare how poets present **identity** in 'Homing' and one other poem from 'Worlds and lives'.

Compare how poets present **the fight against social and political injustice** in 'A Century Later' and one other poem from 'Worlds and lives'.

Compare how poets present **man's relationship with nature** in 'With Birds You're Never Lonely' and one other poem from 'Worlds and lives'.

Compare how poets present **the power of imagination in shaping our relationship with the world** in 'A Portable Paradise' and one other poem from 'Worlds and lives'.

Compare how poets present **heritage** in 'The Jewellery Maker' and one other poem from 'Worlds and lives'.

Compare how poets present **clashes between worlds** in 'Thirteen' and one other poem from 'Worlds and lives'.